Rainbow Rising from a Stream

Rainbow Rising from a Stream

The Natural Way to Well-Being

David K. Reynolds, Ph.D.

QUILL
WILLIAM MORROW
NEW YORK

It is the policy of William Morrow and Company, Inc., and its imprints and affiliates, recognizing the importance of preserving what has been written, to print the books we publish on acid-free paper, and we exert our best efforts to that end.

Library of Congress Cataloging-in-Publication Data

Reynolds, David K.
    Rainbow rising from a stream: the natural way to well-being / David K. Reynolds.
        p. cm.
    ISBN 0-688-11967-0
    1. Morita psychotherapy. 2. Naikan psychotherapy. I. Title.
    RC489.M65R525   1992
        616.89'14—dc20   92-13871
                                                                  CIP

Printed in the United States of America

First Quill Edition

1   2   3   4   5   6   7   8   9   10

BOOK DESIGN BY LISA STOKES

To all those in the third generation of Constructive Living instructors

Foreword

Peak experiences and sudden insights are marvelous spices to human life. But everyday life is not ordinarily composed of such spices; that's what makes them stand out in our minds. Constructive Living is about improving the quality of everyday life. Everyday life brings us moment-by-moment doses of reality. We define our actions in some of those moments as successful and in some others as setbacks. Reality promptly sends us more moments in any case.

The fundamentals of Constructive Living have been spelled out in previous works (*Playing Ball on Running Water; Pools of Lodging for the Moon; A Thousand Waves; Constructive Living; Flowing Bridges, Quiet Waters;* and others). Constructive Living theory draws heavily on the works of two Japanese philosophers and practitioners, Masatake Morita and Ishin Yoshimoto. The former was a psychiatrist who died in the late 1930s, and the latter was a lay therapist who died in 1988. The action aspect of Constructive Living derives in large part from what has come to be called in Japan Morita therapy. The reflection aspect of Constructive Living derives in large part from the practice introduced by Yoshimoto called Naikan, literally "inside observation." Don't be misled by the national origin of these two gentlemen. Their understanding of the everyday life of humans was neither limited to the Japanese nor limited by any Oriental mysticism. Their suggestions remain practical and meaningful, with only slight alterations to fit our modern times and circumstances. And the theory and practice of Constructive Living has been augmented by the careful application of other compatible principles and techniques. The result is a set of consistent suggestions for living sensibly in modern times. These suggestions can be tested experientially. They can be tested in good times and bad, in times of healthy joy and in times of neurotic misery, when making love and when parking the car. Thus they are readily evaluated and readily supported by everyday life experience.

Constructive Living (CL) is about being realistic. The action element of CL advises that feelings (among much of our reality) are uncontrollable directly by the will. We can't turn on and off feelings just by willing them in and out of our lives. So it is realistic to notice them and accept them as part of life, just as we notice our neighbors, some of whom we may like and some of whom we may dislike. Nevertheless we have to get along. Behavior, however, is controllable by our will (except for tics, stuttering, impotence, trembling, and a few other behaviors like these). Moreover, behavior is controllable regardless of our feelings. Behavior is the locus of our freedom. We can be scared to death to fly in a plane and still fly. I am. Feelings are not acceptable excuses for doing or not doing something.

So far we have the fundamental observations that feelings are uncontrollable and that behavior is controllable. What helps us guide our behavior is purpose. We need to be clear on our immediate and long-range purposes so that we know what needs doing. Reality sends us cues about what needs doing if we pay attention and notice them. When there is trash on your lawn, something needs to be done about it; when your child is choking, there is some necessary action; when the car doesn't start, . . . and so forth.

The reflection element of Constructive Living also helps us get a clear perspective on what needs to be done in our lives. Using various techniques that stimulate a more realistic recollection of our past, we come to appreciate the detailed ways we have been supported by others in our everyday lives and find sustained purposes directed toward repaying our debt to the world. Noticing reality and doing something about it are consistent themes within Constructive Living. This book is about ways in which to do just that— pay attention to reality and act on it realistically.

Acknowledgments

I wish to thank the Mental Health Okamoto Memorial Foundation for support during my activities in Japan from 1989 to the present.

My thanks are due also to those who offered quotes and tales and exercises and maxims and other suggestions. I am "gifted" not in the sense of "talented" but in the more accurate sense of being "the recipient of gifts from others." Reality keeps "presenting" me with materials for writing. Sometimes I take without even recognizing that I am borrowing from the efforts of another. This writing is a cooperative "contribution." Your reading is another aspect of the benevolence I receive. Thank you.

There may be misinterpretations or improper emphases in the writing to follow. I am not always sharp to pick up the lessons reality works to teach me, and you. Please accept my apology for the errors. Reality is a much better teacher than I.

Contents
—◄◼►—

Foreword   7
Acknowledgments   11
Introduction   15

Part I: Essays   23
Potential Dangers   25
An Alternate Possibility   27
Challenges   36
Silence   39
On Alcohol and Other Drugs   41
Kids and Meaning   43
Tying Shoelaces as a Spiritual Practice   45
Groom or Gloom   49
Routine Victories   52
Changing Scenes   55
The Appeal of Pessimism   58
A Meaningful Life   60
Theoretical Limits   69
Broad Minds   72
Feelings Are for Feeling   76
Creativity   79
The Perfect Mate   81
I Alone Suffer   84
Identity's Iron Lace   86
Construction and Living   89
Causes   91
Setting the Date   94
Too Soft   96
Guided-Reflection Experience   99

Deliberations on Reflection in Constructive Living   103
Conversations and Correspondence   115

Part II: Applications   123
Maxims   125
Koans   128
Exercises   131
Quiz   139

Part III: Tales of Constructive Living   143
Fluff   145
Hazards of Brilliance   146
Another Chance   147
Grindstone Cowboy   147
Chasing a Phantasm   148
The Dancing Lesson
    by Patricia Ryan-Madson   148
Fairy Tale
    by Sheila Sabrey-Saperstein   150
Trapped   150
Caves   152
The Porcelain Box
    by Patricia Stewart   153
So Darn Cute   154
The Slippery Throat   154
Bite-Sized   155
Weakest Link
    by Daniel Hoppe   156
Sensitivity and Sense   156
Distraction
    by Deanna Kirk   157
Train Tale   157
Entre   158

References   161
Information   163

Introduction

Rain . . . when it relaxes and just lets the drops fall, it is helpful, gentle, nourishing. When it forces the drops down on the world with strong winds, it can be destructive. Just raindrops—now gentle and nourishing, now forced and harmful. Just raindrops.

Perhaps most people take what I write to be simply a strategy for reducing neurotic suffering. But those who look more deeply will find a narrow path of enlightened living wandering among the clumps of wildflowers. The path is not of my construction. It has been there all along. I merely set up markers for those with sharp eyes to follow. Others, too, have erected markers written in Japanese, Arabic, Hebrew, Chinese, and other languages.

Put in different words, there is a stream of consistent advice winding through human history; this book contains raindrop words rising from the stream, as I view them through imperfect eyes.

Individuals with too many miserable moments manifest fascinating characteristics. They may have many regrets; perhaps their greatest regret is that they regret so much. They may lack confidence to generate self-confidence. They worry a lot that they worry a lot. They pile misery on top of misery and bury themselves beneath the mass. And they try to force the rain to fall when and where they please.

I can't help you eliminate all of your suffering. But I know how you can help yourself eliminate a great deal of it. The method is called Constructive Living.

MISCONCEPTIONS

With quite a few books in print about Constructive Living, there has been time and creative imagination for misconceptions to emerge. One might argue that learning about Constructive Living is more accurately a kind of unlearning of misconceptions about life. One misconception about Constructive Living is that its essence is as we have written about it in books. But the essence is the living itself—the doing, the thinking, the feeling. Another misconception is that it takes too long to master, that there are shortcuts that will lead to life satisfacton more quickly and elegantly. "Try, see," the Hawaiians say. This lifeway is difficult, no doubt about it.

Constructive Living has been criticized for its action orientation. "Doing what needs to be done" may appear to be about doing what society or conscience dictates must be done, but it is not. Doing what needs to be done is about the natural, proper, fitting response to what springs from one's environment. The Japanese Moritist phrase *Nasubeki koto nasu* is usually translated as "Do what you must do." There is a sense of obligation in the term *must*. But the real import of the phrase lies in the naturalness or appropriateness of the action. Do what needs doing means fitting one's actions to the situation or circumstance.

Furthermore Constructive Living is not fundamentally Japanese, not psychotherapy, not philosophy, not Zen or Shinshu Buddhism. It holds that unless you have a genuine illness like schizophrenia or a brain tumor, your mind isn't broken, doesn't need to be fixed.

There is a lot to unlearn.

You have been taught that feelings are the most important thing in your life. It isn't so. At the root of many problems in our country is this feeling-focus. The reason why people do drugs is to feel good, as if feeling good (relaxed, confident, happy, at peace, self-loving, transformed, energetic, comfortable, courageous, connected) were the whole of life, worth giving up everything else in life to achieve.

You have been taught that you can "work on" your unpleasant feelings. It can't be done. Not only is it impossible to "work on" your depressed or anxious feelings, you actually have no need to "work on" them. They are terrific! To be sure they are unpleasant and painful, but they have the important function of reminding you that there is something importantly wrong with your life as it is. They won't go away until you have straightened out that problem area of your life. They are like a fever warning you of an infection, a pain warning you of a wound. Constructive Living advises you to get to work on the root cause of the discomfort. Inevitably such work involves changing something you do, changing your behavior.

NOTHING SPECIAL

Recently during the faculty orientation at a well-known retreat facility we were asked to introduce ourselves. As we proceeded around the table, the faculty members described their extraordinary accomplishments and their plans for the upcoming retreat. When my turn came, I introduced myself and stated that I teach people to be ordinary and nothing special. An uproar followed: "How can you teach that? We're already ordinary!"

That's my job. I am selling water to people swimming in a lake. Then why did the World Health Organization send me to the People's Republic of China to teach Constructive Living to psychiatrists? Why are there nearly a hundred certified Constructive Living instructors around the United States, West Germany, Mexico, New Zealand, Japan, and Canada? Why have encouraging articles appeared in *The New York Times, Vogue, New Woman, Men's Health, East West Journal, Cosmopolitan, American Health,* and elsewhere?

My job is to mirror back reality to you. To describe the way things are. My description is couched in words, so it isn't the way things are in fact. Talking about a marathon isn't the same as running one. But the words of Constructive Living don't push you to seek other words in endless loops of concepts that cause you to lose yourself in a domain of verbal abstraction. My words recommend activities that will give you direct experience with reality. You can test their worth.

The authority in Constructive Living is reality, not some Constructive Living dogma. We don't say, "In Constructive Living we tell people they can't control their feelings," or "According to Constructive Living principles . . . ," or "One of the key ideas of Constructive Living is . . . "

Instead we ask, "Can you turn your anger off and on at will?" We invite our students to "try it and see what happens." We point out the undeniable truth that "you can't hit your wife if you're not in the same room with her"; "you have no chance of succeeding on a job interview if you don't show up for the interview."

This kind of commonsense approach requires nothing more than being realistic in the best sense of that word. Constructive Living is not hard to understand. It is sometimes hard to practice. We are sometimes lazy, sometimes perfectionistic, sometimes idealistic, sometimes cowardly, sometimes this and sometimes that. We are not always realistic. Constructive Living helps us take a realistic view of our imperfection, our unrealistic expectations, our flawed world. And we get on with our lives.

I expect that many people will have peak experiences in their lives at one time or another. I can't offer you peak experiences through Constructive Living. Our approach is about everyday life for the most part. So I don't deal in fancy stereos or televisions, just ordinary batteries. Without those ordinary batteries the fancy equipment doesn't function.

In a recent magazine I read in the title of an article the word *humor*. Quickly I turned to the article, anticipating a wry or amusing perspective on the human condition. Instead of humorous anecdotes there was nothing more than the variously repeated advice to have more humor in life. The readers were cheated. Even second-rate jokes offer the chance for a few moments of delight. Do you see the difference between telling someone to be joyful and telling them a funny story? I wonder if the author's suggestion to the home-less this winter is "Be warm!"

MEMBERSHIP CARD

I fear flying. How self-centered my fear of flying is! Of course I fly anyway—to Japan twice a year, to Hawaii, China, New Zealand, around the United States lecturing. As I fly frightened, it is clear that in the neurotic moments I think I am special. My thoughts insist that the plane will crash because I am aboard, because my thinking is negative, because I have failed to live up to my potential. If only I could eliminate flying from my life, I would be satisfied, or so my mind insists in neurotic moments. How foolish and self-focused those moments are! How quicky I forget the efforts of others that keep the plane safely in the skies! How easily I ignore the effects of a potential plane crash on thousands of others besides myself! The focus of attention narrows; the suffering mounts. Then come moments of comparatively reasonable thinking, broader thinking (usually along with periods free of air turbulence). But regardless of the discomfort, I arrive at my destination. I fly.

Sometimes I recognize how easy it would be to dismiss the terror of others as irrational and trivial if it weren't for the periodic reminders of my personal terror in planes. It is my membership card in the club. I really do understand. I really can say that in spite of fear and anxiety we can do what needs doing. That is Constructive Living. Scared to death, I fly.

HISTORICAL ROOTS

Constructive Living was originally inspired by the writings and lives of Masatake Morita and Ishin Yoshimoto, the founders of what are called today Morita therapy and Naikan therapy, respectively. I am sometimes asked what percentage of Constructive Living is Morita, what percentage is Yoshimoto, and what percentage is Reynolds? The unexpected answer is one hundred percent. Morita, Yoshimoto, and I are saying the same thing. We come at our writings from different perspectives and backgrounds and styles. But we are engaged in nothing more than pointing out reality, the way things are.

In a sense Naikan thought provides a map for Constructive Living. Moritist thought provides a vehicle for travel on that map. Naikan answers the questions How can I determine what needs doing? and Why should I do what needs doing? Morita offers advice on the doing. Both Morita and Naikan therapies point us toward practical, concrete, specific, everyday reality. There is so much awesome wonder in that everyday reality if one has eyes to see it.

The world needs only a few people who can see clearly some of the time.

I steal crumbs from a rich banquet table around which only a few sit. Galleries surround the feast. Spectators' mouths water at the sight. They, too, are invited to sit at the table, but they remain in their seats longing, wondering about the flavors and textures arrayed before them. Come sample life's fare!

There's no time like the present.

A SPECIAL NOTE FOR PSYCHOTHERAPISTS

No one seems to believe me when I say that people with formal mental health training may be at a decided disadvantage at learning Constructive Living. Most professionals who hear that message think it's some other mental health professionals to whom I refer. Professional training provides some useful skills, but, on the whole it usually interferes with the learning of Constructive Living. It is a handicap. I have trained psychologists, psychiatrists, clinical social workers, and volunteers on hot lines. I have worked with some of the top names in clinical and research psychology and psychiatry in two countries; so these aren't idle words. Psychotherapy is, of course, a valid professional pursuit. It is not Constructive Living instruction.

Your job requires you to do psychotherapy. Do it well. Regrettably it is unlikely that you can do psychotherapy as your job description requires at this time and do genuine Constructive Living instruction simultaneously. Please do the best you can anyway. Aim to find a way in which your considerable psychotherapeutic skills don't work in conflict with your developing Constructive Living skills. Be wary about offering your psychotherapy-based skills and insights to nonprofessional Constructive Living instructors. However, don't hesitate to offer your Constructive Living–based skills and insights to those nonprofessionals. Be clear about which skills are psychotherapy-based and which are Constructive Living–based.

The people who come to you as patients think you know what you don't know. They think your determined attempts to map the mind provide information that will remove their suffering. How unfortunate for them to misunderstand so radically! But they do come to you. So you want to, you *must,* offer them something beyond the insightful talking that they expect. You owe it to them to provide guidance toward an effective lifeway. Please read on.

The latest Gospel in this world is, Know thy work and do it. "Know Thyself": long enough has that poor "self" of thine tormented thee; thou will never get to "know" it, I believe!

Think it not thy business, this of knowing thyself; thou art an unknowable individual; know what thou canst work at; and work at it, like a Hercules! This will be thy better plan.

Blessed is he who has found his work; let him ask no other blessedness; he has a work, a life-purpose; he has found it and will follow it.

—Thomas Carlyle, *Past and Present*, 1843

PART I

ESSAYS

Potential Dangers

Along the path of Constructive Living there are steep crevasses on both sides. On one side is the danger of falling into some version of the positive-thinking fallacy. Students are lured into trying to create a positive attitude, to generate self-confidence, to discover the plus side of their personalities. They may be enticed into believing that they shouldn't give up hope, that life will produce a door of escape from their dilemma if they trust reality to come through for them. All these seductive attractions share the common trap of positing some precondition for constructive action. They advise you to get confidence first, then it is easier to act positively; first believe, then doors will open; first look on the bright side, then your troubles will appear smaller and you can get on with proper behavior—even your illnesses will be cured!

All such approaches are subtle forms of the fix-your-feelings abyss. Constructive Living holds that there need be no preconditions for constructive activity. Just do it. There is no need to fix the mind; if left alone the mind will function properly (provided it has no true disease, such as a brain tumor or psychosis). It is that very effort to eliminate neurotic moments from the mind that has caused some people to fall into an excess of suffering. Do what is right (not in some narrow moral sense, but what is appropriate, fitting, suitable to the situation), and the mind will take care of itself. There is no need to make a decision or commitment, no need to be empowered, no need to organize oneself or pull oneself together.

It is all right to dwell on past mistakes, to give up hope, to think negatively—while doing mindfully what is right in front of one's nose that needs doing. Morita said that it is all right to give up over and over while climbing a mountain as long as one's feet keep moving upward. The seductive abyss of preparatory or preliminary work on the self holds out the elusive promise of a stronger self (whether it can deliver on the offer is another question). The path of Constructive Living offers a much finer prize—no self at all. In other words it offers involvement in the rich reality that surrounds us and is us, with few distractions from a mind that tries to separate us and distract us from that wealth of real-world stimulation. And the Constructive Living prize isn't to be obtained off in the distance. It is available right now. As you lose yourself in constructive action right now, your neurotic misery disappears. And you increase the chances of getting done the important content of your life. Then when the misery reappears, it is no more than fresh information welling up—now what needs to be done next?

The chasm on the outer side of the Constructive Living path is self-focused too. In its depths lurks the danger of using Constructive Living skills to achieve narrow, selfish purposes. People can use Constructive Living to accept their own driving ambition, greed, their abuse of others. They can become action-oriented and lose sight of humane purposes and goals.

Morita's ideas provide the guardrail that keeps us from falling into the abyss of selfish, feeling-centered living. Naikan provides the guardrail that keeps us from falling into the abyss of soulless living. The path is narrow, but even a few steps along it demonstrate its superiority. Slipping to right and left, we move along, sometimes on hands and knees. On occasion we raise our eyes from the path underfoot and the sturdy guardrails. How kind of reality to provide the chance for a view from the heights!

DAVID K. REYNOLDS

An Alternate Possibility

MYTHS

Constructive Living need not deny that some functions of the mind appear to fit Freudian conceptions of some so-called defense mechanisms. For example, it appears likely that sometimes I see my own feelings and attitudes in others (a sort of projection) and sometimes I am upset at someone or something that, on reflection, may not be the real cause of my upset (a sort of displacement), and sometimes I try to avoid thinking unpleasant thoughts (a kind of suppression), and so forth. However, even if we were to accept uncritically these Freudian contributions to the understanding of the psychological defense mechanisms, we need not endorse the Freudian assumptions about how to deal with them. Achieving some understanding of how our minds work neither gets rid of old habits of thinking and feeling nor eliminates the life problems associated with them.

There was a time when some people believed that talking about one's childhood sexuality was necessary to become free of neurosis. There was a time when some people believed that the trauma of birth needed to be neutralized by some sort of reexperiencing of that event. In more recent times some people believe that salvation lies in discovering past childhood sexual abuse and allowing rage to emerge and be expressed. Salvation doesn't come that cheaply or that simply or that suddenly. Salvation, if such there be, must find itself worked out over and over moment by moment in life's eternal present.

I offer this warning routinely: Beware of anyone who claims to know what you must be feeling, who wants to help you get in touch with feelings that he or she is certain you have but you are not aware of. Simply consider what possible meaning there might be in a phrase like "feelings that aren't felt." Can you have thoughts that aren't thought or beliefs that aren't believed? Long hours of talking and other experiences might eventually produce those stipulated feelings, thoughts, and beliefs. But they weren't there all along unless you actually were feeling, thinking, and believing them in full awareness all along. Uncovering hidden feelings is rather like discovering hidden evil spirits and exorcising them. They don't exist, but if you can convince someone that they do exist, you can charge them to get rid of them. Again, beware of being conned.

I fear that too many of those who do psychotherapy have little life experience outside of educational settings. They have learned to manipulate abstract and theoretical ideas skillfully but have little ability to challenge these ideas in terms of everyday life experience. If you want to get your life together, you might want to look inside the trunk and glove compartment of your therapist's car. If they are crowded and messy, you might wonder how someone who keeps those spaces in disarray can advise you on arranging your life.

CONS

A "con" (or confidence game) is unrelated to truth; sometimes it is true, more often it is not. A con benefits the one who cons. A con *seems* at first to benefit the one who is conned, but in the long run it does him or her harm. Consider the following:

"There's a voice within you that tells you that Constructive Living is true."

"Not in me," says the psychodynamic therapist.

"What denial!" exclaims the Constructive Living instructor, reversing roles with a twinkle in her eye. "Your problem is that *you are not in touch with that voice*. But that's all right; we can work for years, if necessary, until you recognize what I insist you must be hearing."

How foolish to allow others to convince us that they know what we must be hearing or feeling. If you believe that nonsense, then you are probably in the market for magical marital aids and computerized fortune charts. And there is a bridge on the East Coast for sale.

Here is another con. It is easy to find buyers for this philosophy:

You aren't responsible for your overeating (or any harmful behavior). Our goal is to help you assign blame to the hindrances in your past that keep you from being accountable for your overeating. Meanwhile we'll work to help you feel good about yourself while you keep on doing these irresponsible things to your body. At some future time, when you feel comfortable and confident about yourself, you will be able to cut down on your eating with no special effort or discomfort because of your newfound self-love and self-esteem.

What an easy sell that philosophy is! How much of it is actually expensive nonsense dressed up in psychological jargon some people will discover with time and experience.

One final con:

You can feel happy and good about yourself all the time.

Don't believe it. Better yet, check it out for yourself. If there really were someone who could make you feel continually good about yourself, then that might be worth pursuing. But to do so would require that you ignore those times when you shouldn't feel good about yourself—when you were less than your best, when you were hurtful, selfish, thoughtless, stupid. We are all like that sometimes. I wouldn't recommend any practice that requires you systematically to ignore part of reality, even if constant happiness and confidence were possible.

Fortunately there are therapists from a variety of disciplines who aren't limited by rigid theories or thinking. They provide considered, human counseling to troubled clients. If you shop in this area of psychotherapy or counseling, choose carefully.

UNSCIENTIFIC THEORIES

In an important sense psychologists and other psychotherapists are the priests and shamans of the modern world. Troubled people go to them for guidance just as they went to shamans and priests in the past (and some still do today). Counseling and clinical psychology (or related psychiatric practices, for that matter) are not science. However, in this era they must appear to be science in order to have legitimacy and acceptance by the public and by other professionals. The closer psychology actually comes to science (as, for example, in behaviorism and behavior therapy), the more trivial and more divorced it becomes from the human mind and the complex human problems of living.

Again, there are few, if any, truly scientific theories in psychology. But there are many attempts to explain and understand the human mind and human behavior. Such attempts should not be confused with scientific theories. Nevertheless, explanations have their uses, whether they are scientific or not. If clients believe an explanation, they have some sense of having a handle on their problems, a course to follow to solve their difficulties. Constructive Living is not scientific either; it is experiential. You can trust your own experience more than you can trust someone else's theory, any theory, including Constructive Living theory. We CL practitioners can construct theories as well as the next fellow, as is shown shortly below. But we keep directing our students toward examining their own experience with reality rather than asking them to believe our explanations of the sources of their life dilemmas.

I suspect that it isn't necessary to have a particularly elaborate theory of the mind. The endeavor to make a grand theory of the human mind seems to me little more than trying to wrap the mind in more idea paper.

DAVID K. REYNOLDS

If neurotic suffering is an illness, then it is a strange kind of illness. It is not caused by a virus or bacteria; there is no trauma involved. It is not an organic problem at all, but a "functional" problem.

Can there be an illness of bad humor or stubbornness or laziness? Recent attempts to make shyness and exhaustion illnesses show us the extremes to which medical-sounding classifications can go.

If pseudomedical diagnoses become too broad, applying to behaviors and even concepts (like the concept "society"), then the meaning of illness is diluted to the point of meaninglessness.

As far as I can see, the only people who profit from maintaining a label of illness in reference to fears and guilt and cowardice and timidity and obsession and sadness and abusing alcohol and other drugs and the like are those who call themselves "therapists" or "healers"—physicians and clinical psychologists, for example. There is no genuine advantage to being a "patient" unless there are medications or other treatment modalities that are known to bring about "cure." Neurosis isn't cured. It is outgrown or endured, like an elder sibling's clothes.

PSYCHODYNAMICS AND CONSTRUCTIVE LIVING

Traditional psychodynamic theory offers explanations for a variety of feelings, thoughts, and behaviors. Some people mistakenly believe that psychodynamic theory is the only theory available. Constructive Living theory is a viable alternative with much to offer: for example, it doesn't postulate hidden unconscious sources, it is readily understandable, it can be verified scientifically and by personal experience, it offers immediate practical applications, and it requires no arcane skills or long years of therapy to produce results.

Let's consider a not-too-uncommon phenomenon and compare the explanations offered by a psychodynamically oriented theory with those of Constructive Living. In the past I was part of a team investigating psychological problems in the aftermath of major disasters. We studied and offered help to the victims of earthquakes, floods, tornadoes, and the like. On occasion we would encounter someone who made it through the immediate crisis following the disaster and then became emotionally upset a year or so later. For example, one man reacted to a Colorado flood by immersing himself in the tasks of helping others, filling out paperwork, cleaning up the debris, and so forth. Then, about a year later, he broke down crying when he was unable to find a parking space.

Put simply, psychodynamic theory holds that because the flood victim didn't express his feelings of rage, terror, grief, and the like during the flood and its immediate aftermath, the feelings lurked in his unconscious until some minor frustration (no parking space, in this case) allowed them to erupt a year later. The principle is that unless expressed, feelings build up and cause difficult outbursts later. One problem with such an explanation is that it is impossible to determine whether it is true; there is no way to verify the existence of unconscious feelings, no way to disprove the theory. Another problem is that people who do express feelings during the disaster sometimes suffer from emotional outbursts a year or more later as well. In fact you may know someone who expresses feelings to such a degree that he or she seems to build up stronger and stronger emotions in the process. Rather than "getting the feelings out" and thus eliminating them somehow (according to psychodynamic theory), the person seems to be generating more anger or fear or whatever feeling. The implicit model offered by psychodynamic theory is that of a steam boiler. Feelings build up until they must be released through some pressure valve. One wonders how the release of pressure can build up more pressure in some people and why some people seem to be operating with less pressure than others.

An alternate view of the man who cried when no parking space was available is offered by Constructive Living. We begin by denying that he must have been feeling some assumed feelings during and immediately following the flood. He may have had moments of terror, rage, grief and so forth; but he may have had moments of relief, caring, satisfaction, and accomplishment as well. In the after-

DAVID K. REYNOLDS

math of the flood he focused on getting certain tasks done. Constructive Living recommends noticing and acknowledging feelings when they appear but not digging around for feelings that someone else tells us must be there. The reason why feelings should be acknowledged is because they are part of our immediate reality. Reality is worth noticing, acknowledging. We don't need to probe for (presumed) hidden feelings in order to exorcise them. Perhaps the man did acknowledge his feelings at the time, perhaps not. Most likely he sometimes did, sometimes didn't.

Now we come to the fact of the tears when no parking space was available. How can we explain them without assuming they reflect some eruption of unconscious feelings? Constructive Living theory holds that feelings fade over time unless restimulated by actions or events. So the explanation is that during the year following the disaster the man's upset diminished until the frustration of parking caused him to recall the frustrations and upset of the disaster. He may have remembered the helplessness and panic he felt during the flood. New feelings welled up to provoke tears. There is no need to postulate some earlier feelings lurking in his unconscious (wherever that might be) during all these months. Every feeling is a new feeling, just as every moment is a fresh one, emerging from and into reality.

You see, the Constructive Living explanation doesn't require you to believe in some mysterious, unverifiable unconscious. You can verify whether feelings fade over time unless restimulated by actions or events. Check your own experience and you will find that it is so. I hold that you can make Constructive Living sense of any thought, feeling, or behavior. And the explanation offered by Constructive Living will make at least as much sense, and will be more practically useful, than psychodynamic explanations.

Beware of stories about strange thoughts and behaviors that seem to require psychodynamic interpretations. The storytellers may give you only the parts of the story that they noticed or need in order to fit their theories. Just keep your eyes on reality and decide for yourself what makes the best sense of it.

CONCLUSION

Constructive Living provides a genuine alternative model for Western psychotherapy's models of human suffering and successful living. Constructive Living doesn't merely substitute a new form of understanding human behavior to replace entrenched Western psychological explanantions. Constructive Living argues that human behavior cannot and need not be explained by some postulated concept called the unconscious. Our approach is not irresponsible, it is not nihilistic, it is not hopeless. It merely suggests that our students' experience is more trustworthy than some scholars' words. As Richard Wilhelm (1985) put it, "Lao Zi (Lao Tsu) does not make scientifically verifiable statements about (the Way). Given the nature of the issue, he cannot offer proof but he points to ways in which one may come to the experience of (the Way)." This strategy is the same as that adopted by Constructive Living. We offer enough information and exercises for you to check out the validity for yourself.

In fact Constructive Living offers testable assertions against which you can compare your own life history. Constructive Living argues that you won't find any of the following conditions in reality, but if you could, they would comprise a disproof of parts of Constructive Living theory:

- If you can control your feelings with consistency simply by willing feelings to change . . .
- If you stay on the same level of Constructive Living development without advancing or declining in your ability to live life well . . .
- If the world isn't supporting you in concrete, specific ways . . .
- If no one fed and clothed you as a child . . .
- If you continue to suffer to the same degree even when distracted or engrossed in the task at hand . . .
- If your feelings don't fade over time in the absence of restimulating events . . .
- If the most satisfying times in your life don't include times with behavioral accomplishments . . .

DAVID K. REYNOLDS

If any of the foregoing conditions apply in your life, you have discovered an inconsistency in Constructive Living theory. The list could easily be extended. Read through this and other Constructive Living books and generate your own list of testable assertions and check out their validity for yourself.

Enough of such talk. On with other aspects of living.

Challenges

We may struggle with our spouse, our mother-in-law, cancer, old age, neurotic symptoms, insomnia, but we have to learn to get along with them too.

We wake up in the middle of the night and try to rediscover the pinpoint of sleep on the broad plain of awareness. Then we try to fit our mind through that slumber dot. How difficult that goal may be to achieve! The more we struggle and try to force sleep, the farther it recedes. Not only sleep resists our pressure of course.

Accepting feelings or other aspects of reality doesn't mean passive behavior. But active behavior doesn't necessarily imply struggle either. Challenges.

Sometimes I take walks around the small Empire Lakes in Coos Bay. A few other people may be doing the same, sometimes in the opposite direction. When we pass the first time, there is a natural opportunity for a greeting, but what about twenty minutes later when we pass again? There is a moment of social awkwardness. Some people have had the experience enough to develop regular responses like "Haven't I seen you somewhere before?" delivered with a smile. Or just a nod of recognition.

Constructive Living instructors, too, encounter emotional situations and develop accustomed responses to them. I used to think that the skills I had learned over the years in dealing with angry or suicidal or anxious or dying students had solved my own emotional responses to these situations. Certainly I wasn't so caught up in the students' feelings as to lose my ability to produce some considered response. But such a repertoire of therapeutic responses doesn't remove the discomfort of the instructor when facing an upset student. The feelings may occur during or after the session. That is just as it should be. Experiential knowledge may give us the ability to do what needs doing in emotional situations, but it doesn't eliminate the emotions. It is natural to feel upset when faced with an upset friend or relative or client. It is natural to feel awkward in an awkward social situation, tense in tense circumstances, shocked in shocking predicaments.

No amount of skill will remove our emotional reactions to disturbing or exciting stimuli. Skills may help us act appropriately, and they may distract us from attending solely to emerging feelings. But emotions are natural products of the contexts of our lives, *are* our very lives in some moments; so emotions cannot, need not, should not be controlled or eliminated—even the most agitating ones. Emotions provide information about our world; to diminish them would be like wearing blinders.

Beware! What you call depression may be sluggishness from lack of exercise. If your physical health permits, take a brisk walk and see if your mood lifts. A regular program of exercise may solve a major portion of your blues. Feelings send us important messages about what needs to be done in our lives. Don't forget that they are NOT the ONLY messages; they should not be the only determinants of our behavior. So working to "fix" feelings, instead of working to notice them and understand their messages, is a mistake. Their signals are important information. Who would want to remove traffic signals from the streets even though sometimes they are inconveniently red?

We joust with phantoms. We wrestle with shadows. We stalk illusions. We seek to put clouds in cardboard boxes to store in the attics of our lives.

Just this-here-now. Simply not-so-simple. Yet another challenge? Struggling again?

DAVID K. REYNOLDS

Silence

It seems to me that people keep burying their thoughts under a deluge of information input. Many people turn on the radio in their car or at home or at work and leave it on as a sort of defense against listening to their own thoughts. What their own minds might churn up is for them frightening or uninteresting, without value. Television and novels serve the same purpose of distraction for some.

One of the privileges of being a writer is that long periods are spent quietly with one's own mind. A kind of intimacy develops in the silence. One learns the mind's foibles and strengths. Perhaps one cannot develop such an intimacy with one's mind while watching television or conversing or playing football. Isolation and silence are necessary. Meditation offers such benefits; so do long, private walks in the woods.

Getting to know ourselves in secluded surroundings in silence is a worthwhile endeavor. We discover facets that never turn up by the light of a video screen.

In our extended association with television, film, and radio we suffer from a distortion of time. We live vicariously through the characters of dramas and comedies. We suffer their pain and adopt their solutions to their adversities. We are exposed to a wide span of life problems and remedies, more than any other people at any other time. But these media-housed difficulties emerge and their resolutions take place within hours. We may come to expect rapid relief of our own life predicaments too. The pace of our lives cannot accelerate to equal that of the media.

The fog softens the view from my Coos Bay window this morning. The greens gradually shift to grays and browns and white. By afternoon the fog bank will soundlessly recede over the ocean again, and damp leaves will glisten silver green. Just notice and appreciate what is there and wait for the inevitable change. Dip into timelessness.

On Alcohol and Other Drugs

My basic objection to alcohol and other drugs is that they interfere with our perception of reality. Constructive Living is about living the best one can within reality. Reality may not be what we wish or what we believe ought to be. But stuffing our minds in some idealized or fantasized space for long periods doesn't help us cope with or change reality. In fact teasing oneself with alcohol and other drugs may result in very real consequences, such as auto accidents, poor job performance, and broken homes. You know that.

The other danger of these chemical pursuits of unreality is that they encourage feeling-centeredness. They may make one feel good, temporarily. So they encourage the user to try to build life on feelings. We know that feelings are not controllable directly by the will. Therefore a feeling-centered life is always in jeopardy; it can't be successfully lived with consistency. Sometimes we feel good, even ecstatic, sometimes not. Up and down, up and down.

Behavior is controllable, no matter what you hear from alcoholics and addicts. They can stop. And the stopping itself demonstrates to them and to us the freedom we all share. With that freedom comes the chance to live a life based on something controllable, stable. There won't be the momentary chemical highs of the past, and there won't be the desperate, urgent, helpless suffering in between. There is no once-and-for-all-time decision involved here. There aren't even a lot of daily decisions. There is just doing something else besides abusing chemicals. The result is simply the satisfaction of living this moment well, and this moment, and this moment.

Kids and Meaning
—◄◄◉►►—

Too many kids don't know what to do these days. They don't know what is worth doing. They see what their parents are doing. They see what their teachers are doing. They see what their friends are doing. Still they don't know what to do.

So people try to attract these kids' attention in order to tell them what to do. The ads that flash brightest, the music albums and videos that shout loudest, whatever stimuli are shocking and exciting—all these get their attention but don't offer anything much worth doing. Just trivial things such as "Buy this, buy that, get rich, travel."

If kids take drugs, they don't have to worry about what to do. The decision dilemma disappears. The only thing worth doing for those kids is getting drugs.

I don't get letters from kids. Mail comes from people in their late twenties and older. Why do you suppose? Only then do many people start wondering about what is really worth doing in their lives. Only then do they begin to realize the importance of the issues raised and the solutions presented by Constructive Living. Very late . . .

We have extended childhood and adolescence in the United

States (and in Japan) into the twenties and even the thirties. But valuable attributes of truth, confidence, and pride come from mature action as an adult even while giving up some of the fun of childhood. We have gained the immediate amusements of childhood, but at the expense of the delights of adult accomplishment.

It's time to grow up.

Tying Shoelaces as a Spiritual Practice

There are many ways to tie shoelaces—bow knots, double bow knots, square knots, granny knots, and so forth. The tying of the knot is a spiritual practice, whatever knot is used. Whether the knot is tied mindfully or not, whether the knot is tied with recognition that the act is spiritual or not, the act is, nevertheless, spiritual. Every act is so. There is no element that can be added onto an act to make it spiritual. Moreover nothing need be added to an act to make it spiritual. All acts are spiritual just as they are.

Reality cannot be divided conceptually into spiritual and non-spiritual categories to any useful end. It is all sacred. It is all holy. Reality is what it is; recognize it or not, the cricket is chirping, the cars roar past the window.

Why, then, do we encourage mindful, attentive action? If it isn't the mindfulness that makes an act holy, if any method of shoelace tying is a sacred act, why go to the trouble to tie shoes well, with full attention? The answer is simple: Holy activities deserve to be recognized as such. We can ignore the pain that our births caused our mothers, but the pain existed nevertheless. We can thoughtlessly slam the car into gear or ease it gently into gear with grateful attention, but the car continues to serve us.

So if you walk inside an edifice and voices become hushed and faces show awe and reverence, those voices and faces show how carelessly their owners view the reality outside that edifice. Nowhere is holier than anywhere else. It is all holy—the shoelaces, the temples, the cricket, the cars—all of it.

Our eyes don't make reality holy, our actions don't make reality holy, it simply *is* that way. How reassuring! Because sometimes we forget.

Once I bought a hair dryer as a birthday gift for a friend on the very day her old hair dryer broke. The next day as I was riding a train, I had a premonition that a nearby passenger would spill something on my slacks, and she did. The Japanese call such occurrences *fushigi*. That word can be translated as "marvelous" or "wondrous." Our everyday lives are filled with marvelous events, but we take them for granted. Where do the fresh moments we experience come from? Where do our thoughts come from? Where do the words we speak come from? Where does the rich variety of reality come from? How is it that reality provides this particular chair for my comfort, this air conditioner, this word processor, these slippers? The vast efforts of others on our behalf are readily discovered with a little reflection, but they are nonetheless marvelous. It is this sense of wonder about ordinary life that characterizes the student of Constructive Living. As we have seen, there is no religious separation of life into the holy and mundane—Sabbath and weekday, priest and layperson, worship and work, prayer and conversation, temple and house. It is all holy, if you wish to use such a term.

I want to put the mystery and transcendence back into our perception of everyday reality, where it belongs. We can only see reality as "ordinary" by ignoring its magnificence. And so I resist making Constructive Living into a form of therapy, like Morita therapy and Naikan therapy. I want these ideas to be natural, normal parts of everyday life—not set apart as special techniques applicable only to the neurotic.

Religion, too, has too much become the domain of the "set apart." For the most part the institutionalized religions of our day have become talk shows with ministers and priests in hierarchies

DAVID K. REYNOLDS

of talk-show hosts. Religious practitioners talk too much about talking. Too little do they talk about experiencing their faith; too little do they ground their beliefs in everyday reality.

My second fundamental quarrel with organized religion has to do with its divisiveness. In the first place religion tends to divide the world into that which is holy or sacred and that which is ordinary, secular, mundane. Even in some Zen centers (*center* is a term much preferable to *temple*), where people should know better, there is an attitude of reverence and awe as members enter the zendo where zazen meditation takes place. That same attitude isn't exhibited when entering the dining room or cars or the toilet. That's a fundamental mistake fostered by religion. All of reality is worthy of our deep respect.

A similar divisiveness separates humans themselves into sacred and secular categories and into hierarchies within those categories. Certain roles are created that are set apart and (however it may be denied) set above other roles. These roles are signified by special titles and dress—often the colors of robes have hierarchical significance. Leaders are served as though they alone were representatives of superior beings (God, Buddha, and so on).

Such religious pigeonholing promotes the notion that the sacred is to be approached in certain places at certain times through the good offices of certain chosen people. But the sacred is around you, is you, all the time, is time.

"Once, the church understood this; there must be a perpetual mysticism, perpetual experience. . . .'Pray without ceasing' means pray *now*, in the present moment" (quoted from the journal of Father Sylvan in Jacob Needleman, 1980).

"What, then, is the Constructive Living attitude toward 'higher truths'?" you may ask. Unfortunately should you present such a query, I would have no idea what you were asking. Which truths are higher than others? If you are talking about truths that cannot be tested by experience in ordinary reality, then I suspect that you have no idea what you are asking. Robert Heinlein expressed similar views in *To Sail Beyond the Sunset*. Watch out for people who talk about untestable spiritual truths, he warned, they are after your money. And, "Eventually I learned that the Church is run solely for the benefit of the priesthood, not for the good of our people." And, again, "'But you must respect another man's religious beliefs!' for Heaven's sake, why? Stupid is stupid—faith doesn't make it smart."

Having read all the above criticism, don't get the idea that I am against religion altogether. I simply oppose the thoughtless, automatic, self-serving religion that interferes with the genuine needs of humans to see beyond themselves. Both Morita and Yoshimoto, the founders of Morita therapy and Naikan therapy respectively, recognized that their approaches brought serious students to the doorway of true religious experience, whatever form it might take for the individual. They were right. Constructive Living, based on their insights, offers the same opportunity.

"I'm not talking about a theory among theories but about the way things are."

"That sounds like religious talk to me."

"Then you are fortunate. If your religion talks about the real world, it is rare. Most don't."

Groom or Gloom

Appearance isn't everything, but it is something. Have you ever thought there was no need to shave or put on makeup one morning because no one was going to see you that day anyway? Have you ever failed to comb or brush your hair because you felt so miserable? Have you ever lounged around in robe and slippers well into the afternoon? I want to present here two different perspectives on why such practices are wrong; the perspectives come from the reflection and action aspects of Constructive Living.

You may have read the Moritist maxim, Behavior wags the tail of feelings. In Constructive Living we point out that our actions influence how we think and feel. Because what we do is the most controllable aspect of our lives (even more controllable than thinking), we use our actions to provide the steady groundwork for building our lives. Although we may not feel like keeping ourselves well groomed, we can do it (within the limits of any physical handicaps we might have of course). From this perspective, keeping ourselves spruced up is simply something that needs doing. It will have an effect on other features of our lives.

The issue of hypocrisy may arise here. Aren't we lying to others when we put on a good face even when feeling miserable or lazy?

Isn't it better to be true to ourselves? Underlying these questions is the issue of untruth for personal gain at the expense of others. That sort of hypocrisy isn't what concerns us here. Grooming ourselves is just doing the best we can in a given situation. The fact of the matter is that we may find our feelings changing to fit our new face. Conversely, sloppy attire and an unwashed face may provoke more gloom.

Here is a different perspective on maintaining a pleasant appearance: Whatever its effect on us, the world deserves it. What you are about to read may appear strange, but I ask you to consider it with an open mind. Let's start with the most acceptable argument. Maybe your spouse has seen you looking terrible before and he or she loves you anyway. But your spouse deserves to see you looking clean and unrumpled. Consider your appearance a sort of gift, an initial payment on a loan from a loved one you need to work at paying off. Taken a step farther, there is the chance that someone else might see you or telephone you—a postal carrier, perhaps, or a neighbor. And your voice on the phone might be influenced by your attire and personal grooming.

Again, this line of thought has nothing to do with the effects of a neat appearance on you, but it is about the effects of how you look on the world around you. Now comes the step that might seem odd: Even if no one has any direct contact with you at all that day, the furniture and walls and magazines and dishes and washbasin and wastebasket and all those objects around you deserve to see you looking your best. But they have no eyes! Right. And they are just things; they haven't earned any special treatment! Partly right; they are things. Whether or not they deserve special treatment depends on your point of view. It would be hard to argue that your washbasin and wastebasket haven't been useful to you in the past. And it might be convenient to ignore their service just because they don't move around on their own and talk. It might be convenient to classify a large part of reality as "objects" that don't merit thoughtful recognition for service and so don't merit any return from us. Our debts are reduced quite simply that way, rather like the imaginative notion of doing away with the national debt by legally abolishing it. Think about it.

So we've considered this issue of grooming from a couple of angles. One way to check out the value of these suggestions is to verify them through experience. The investment is likely to be worth your while.

Routine Victories

Variety adds spice to life. Some people seem to be obsessed with variety, however, and miss the benefits of a steady, familiar routine. Routines can help us refine our skills of daily living.

Routine frees up our attention to explore in more depth what it is we are about. In every monastic tradition I know of there is great reliance on routine. Routine allows for looking at details and increasing awareness. Of course routine doesn't guarantee such benefits. We can drift into automatic, mindless ritual. But the gross changes that require our shifting and stimulated attention in new situations don't ordinarily interfere within the bounds of reasoned habit.

Another benefit of routine is that it permits a standard for comparison, a measure of progress or problems. There is meaning in minor changes. Deviations from the accustomed path offer subtle information about what needs doing next. When I see students in individual sessions, I follow a pretty consistent pattern from session to session. There is so little time together that I need all the clues I can get in order to be able to offer the best instruction.

Systematic practices of behavior keep materials in their proper places ready for use. Putting away tools in their proper places makes them available when needed next. It's common sense. We benefit from predictability and order.

Procedures of custom help us build incrementally on past experience. Routine allows us to deepen our skills and techniques, and it permits us to notice and improve the setting in which we operate.

Routine offers others knowledge of your activities so that they can plan theirs better. Most Constructive Living instructors know that I am writing in the early morning and go to bed early at night. They thoughtfully time their telephone calls accordingly.

To be sure, routine must be tempered with flexibility. Our goal is not rigidity. There are two kinds of practice. One is rote practice, doing the same thing over and over again. The second is enlightened practice, action that keeps adapting to changing situations and building on experience. I suspect we need a solid base of behavioral habit in order to get maximum benefits from considered, reasoned flexibility. People who drift too much don't seem to accomplish much with their lives. Routine helps us get done those difficult but necessary tasks of living. Habits provide a psychological path for preparing the mind for all sorts of activities. For example, my morning customs facilitate the smooth transition from bed to standing here in front of this word processor. It's early; if I sit down I get sleepy. If I allow time for reflecting on whether to write or not this morning, it might be necessary to invest effort in overcoming resistance to writing. Nearly all the time there are lots of things I would rather do than write. But writing needs doing. My morning routine helps get it done.

Particularly for the bright, perfectionistic, idealistic, sensitive, introverted, ruminating, obsessing, self-critical people we call shinks (from the Japanese word *shinkeishitsu*), the increased orderliness of stimuli generated by routine behavior offers some appreciated relief from dealing with a stimuli-rich environment. Shinks' minds are pretty constantly active during their waking moments.

Routine helps provide information about which stimuli need attention at the moment and which don't.

In a world that keeps advertising the benefits of the new, the exotic, the fast-paced, and the disposable, we do well not to forget the dependable routine.

Changing Scenes

ON THE ROAD

Travelers are given a special opportunity to recognize the kindness and service of others in their behalf. The simplest needs must be provided by others in noticeable, unmistakable ways. This night's lodging, food, toilet facilities, and social contact come from the efforts of my host. It is no wonder that monks and devout laypeople in many countries had traditions of religious journeying, pilgrimage.

The reminders of others' labor come often for me. I travel a lot presenting the lore of Constructive Living. But no matter how far I travel, each night when I sleep, I am home again.

As I travel across the country, change is accelerated and magnified. I wake up to different sorts of morning weather; I drive through storm fronts. The land and sky keep shifting. The taste of water changes, too, from place to place. The local foods and prices and ways of speaking change as well.

We travelers exchange information. We talk about road conditions and good places to stop—places to eat or look or stay the night, places to avoid. We use maps created by people we have never met. My dependence on these strangers is noticeable. How kind of them to share their hard-won information!

Travel forces me to recognize the importance of good health in life. I don't enjoy a scenic spot as much when my stomach is upset or appreciate a good meal as much when my head hurts. Poor road conditions are easier to endure when my body is functioning well.

Travel tests the limits of our endurance; tells us about our needs. It allows us to experiment with new customs, new language, new identities. And traveling allows us to come home.

"Welcome home!" I remember well in all my Pacific travels the first time an official of Customs and Immigration greeted returning American passengers at Honolulu International Airport with these words. Thinking of myself as a citizen of the world, I was surprised to feel my eyes mist with tears.

We can learn these lessons at home, I suppose. But traveling brings them home to us and with us.

ON THE MOVE

Not so long ago we moved from Los Angeles to Coos Bay, Oregon. Because we planned to maintain an office in Los Angeles, it was necessary to decide what should be moved and what should be bought new, what should be packed and what should be left behind. It reminds me of going on a trip. I had to consider essentials.

Along with the benefits of having a house and garage and yard came the worries of expenses, maintenance, security. Owning more means having more to lose, or so it seems. Delight brings the fear of losing the delight; success brings worries about sustaining the success. Good health brings concerns about losing it. The neurotic side of us finds the dark shadows surrounding every patch of sunlight.

Constructive Living advises us to notice the sunlight and the shadows, to accept them both. What other course is possible? To try to eliminate the sunlight would only darken our lives. To ignore the shadows is both unrealistic and impossible. To go beyond sunlight and shadow may be possible for a select few, but even for them the path must go through acceptance of what is.

We have been assembling furniture. How impressive when the carton of pieces and screws and dowels becomes a desk or a bookcase! When I fail to follow the instructions, the holes don't line up properly, extra parts remain, the result is unstable. Then I must redo the work properly. Of course. When I have failed to do my life well, what can be redone must be redone satisfactorily. It is only natural. Nothing special.

There are so many details involved in moving. Car registration, driver's license, electricity, water, phone, bank account, trash pickup, mail forwarding, post office box, insurance, arranging for lawn care while I'm traveling, furniture, shopping, and so on. I cannot keep all these details in mind. A checklist helps. It is troublesome to stop in the midst of activity to write something on the checklist. But it isn't *stopping* in the midst of activity to do so, is it? Writing is just more activity in the midst of activity. Now carrying in the groceries, now buying the lamp, now adding to the checklist, now chopping wood, now opening a new checking account.

It takes time to settle in. One doesn't feel "at home" at once. The countless doings over time make a home or a job or a physical disability familiar. We get accustomed to the positive and negative aspects of the situation. Over and over we see the signs of our presence, the marks of our existence. There's no rush. Again, nothing special.

The Appeal of Pessimism

I can see two attractions of pessimism. Firstly, when things go wrong, at least the pessimists can claim they expected the worst and they were right. Secondly, on television and in movies just when life goes well for the hero, just when misfortune is unexpected, something terrible happens. There may be some expectation among pessimists that always anticipating the worst can magically prevent unfortunate events from occurring. Both of these measures aim at cutting anticipated losses, losses that might not even occur. But such a purpose is the basis of any insurance. The problem with pessimism is that the premiums are very high.

Of course, strictly speaking, there are no pessimists, only people who have frequent moments of pessimism. No one can be negative all the time. And everyone has moments of expecting the worst. Habits of attitude aren't easily changed. Constructive Living suggests we use the information our minds send us, however negative or unpleasant, to assist us in behaving positively and constructively. If you worry that your roof might be leaking, check it. If you feel gloomy about your job prospects, work to improve them.

We do, however, sometimes feel pessimistic about conditions we can't do anything about. If you know something about Constructive Living, then you can guess the approach we recommend in such situations. When you can't do anything to change the circumstances, then you accept the circumstances, you accept the pessimistic feelings associated with them, you accept your dislike of feeling pessimistic, you accept your dissatisfaction with all this accepting, you accept your tendency to analyze this whole situation. And meanwhile you get on with doing what can be done in your life. Optimistic or pessimistic, clever or foolish, thoughtful or thoughtless, eager or reluctant, active or passive—we are all of these at one moment or another. Constructive Living won't make you optimistic; it doesn't need to do so. Just doing well what reality sends to be done is sufficient. Issues of optimism and pessimism and the like will wither away from inattention.

A Meaningful Life

[The following chapter, in slightly different form, was originally presented as lectures at Meaningful Life Therapy (MLT) conferences in Kurashiki and Hamamatsu, Japan, in 1989 and 1990. Meaningful Life Therapy uses Moritist principles and other methods to improve the quality of lives of patients with long-term illnesses, particularly cancer patients. For more details read my book *A Thousand Waves* (Morrow, 1990). The audiences consisted of cancer patients and their families, medical and nursing and other support staff.]

DISCOVERING POSITIVE ELEMENTS

We tend to think only of the negative aspects of certain natural parts of our world. We think of pain and stress and anxiety and illness as absolutely bad. Now, they certainly aren't pleasurable. They bring us discomfort. We try to avoid them of course. What I want to point out here is that pain and stress and anxiety and illness cannot be absolutely avoided; they are built into human existence and for some significant reasons. One of the ways to make them more endurable is to achieve a more balanced recognition of their natural and positive aspects.

Please consider this point carefully. I am not suggesting we should learn to love pain or stress. I am not suggesting that we should stop working to minimize discomfort in our lives. No matter what I wrote, no one (including myself) would come to desire discomfort. What I am contending is that the discomfort we feel sometimes spurs us to do important things in our lives, and sometimes there are more important things for us to do than fight against discomfort.

Pain, illness, stress, and anxiety get our attention. They signal us that something is wrong. They tell us that something needs to be done. You know, of course, that people who cannot feel pain suffer from all sorts of dangerous injuries because their bodies don't warn them that something is wrong. They can cut themselves and bleed to death or break a limb and continue to use it without noticing that anything is wrong. Similarly, the uncomfortable symptoms of an illness alert us to the presence of invading organisms or other unhealthy conditions. Anxiety and feelings of stress draw our attention to problems in ourselves and in the rest of our environment.

All of these unpleasant signs (illness, stress, anxiety, pain) point us toward conditions in our world that require our attention. Without these signs we wouldn't be able to respond appropriately to our reality. The unfortunate thing is that sometimes these signals alert us but we cannot find something appropriate to do in order to correct the situation. Anxiety may force us to notice a problem in our marriage or job, but we cannot think of anything to do to correct the problem. The symptoms of an illness may point us to the need for medical treatment, but there may be no effective therapy at this time and level of medical science. Pain may be inescapable unless there is some sacrifice of alertness and movement. Sometimes the signal is there, but we cannot find a proper way to respond to its message. We are prompted by these circumstances to choose.

I believe that in our lives there are more times when we know what needs doing and don't do it than there are times when we know there is a problem but cannnot find anything to do about it. So the first priority of Constructive Living is to help people get on with sensitively and sensibly fixing what can be fixed in their lives, to respond to the pleasant and unpleasant messages that reality sends their way, to live as fully as they can. The next priority is to develop an attitude of acceptance toward the parts of life that can't be fixed.

Again, please read carefully here. I am not arguing for giving up and accepting illness or pain or stress or anxiety as long as there is something that can be done about them. Meaningful Life Therapy teaches a wonderful attitude toward illness—challenging, active, positive. The more patients involve themselves in living fully, the less attention they have to focus on and complain about discomfort. On the simplest level Meaningful Life Therapy and Constructive Living offer relief through distraction from misery. And sometimes, while living actively, the source of their medical problem is solved, and they get well. But there is another level as well.

ACCEPTANCE

What cannot be changed must be accepted. That is the same important truth one finds in the prayer of Alcoholics Anonymous. Constructive Living suggests, further, that what can be changed must be accepted too. Acceptance and action to change can go on at the same time. You don't need to choose one or the other. All of reality must be accepted. Here is the pain, yes, that's the way it is, now what can I do about it? Here is the cancer, yes, reality has brought me cancer, now what can I do about it? Here is the job loss, the breakup, the death of a loved one; what needs to be done?

It is terrible to be faced with a problem that seems to have no solution. It is even worse to torture yourself with ruminations about what should have been done, if only you hadn't, wishes about what might have been, criticism of yourself and others. Accepting the reality of a situation is an important step toward doing something about it. Denial, a long-term focus on feelings, and obsessing on the unfairness of it all simply work to make more misery.

"All right. Here I am. I don't like it. It hurts. But that's the way it is right now. What needs doing?" That chain of thinking is a healthy response to an unpleasant circumstance. Reality will continue to present you with "tasks," as we in Constructive Living call them. We may call what reality brings anything we like. We label the events in our lives "tragedies," "successes," "nightmares," "triumphs," "challenges," "defeats," and so forth. Reality doesn't mind, It just keeps on presenting us with information that deserves our attention and action. What we do about what reality brings us is up to us.

PURPOSE AND FREEDOM

Nanto naku is a Japanese phrase meaning "without reason" or "without goal." It is the phrase a Japanese person uses when he doesn't know the answer to someone's question, "Why did you do that?" "Gee, I don't know; it just seemed like the thing to do (*nanto naku*)." *Nanto naku* is how nonhuman animals live all the time, instinctually. We humans can live purposefully. Purposefully is not always naturally. It is in the interface between purpose and nature that our freedom and our misery are born. The illness of cancer is natural. Our distress, our pain, our fear of dying are all natural. But so is our desire to fight our illnesses, our desire to survive, to be useful to others in the midst of our afflictions. They are natural too.

Our purposes make us human. Yet our natural circumstances may interfere with the accomplishment of our purposes. It is in the dynamic tension between our purposes and natural limits that we are challenged to live fully. Our purposes will help determine which parts of the natural world we focus on and which parts we set on a back shelf much of the time.

Again, I don't say that illness is wonderful. But it provides us with the occasion to notice our purposes, to make new and viable purposes, to struggle to achieve our purposes. It is another aspect of living, with its own limits and possibilities and new opportunities to develop constructive lives.

It is very important to distinguish between (a) brushing your teeth in order to get your teeth clean and gums stimulated; (b) brushing your teeth in order to diminish your anxiety about having unbrushed teeth; (c) brushing your teeth in order to please someone else; (d) brushing your teeth out of habit; (e) brushing your teeth as a spiritual practice; and (f) brushing your teeth in order to achieve some elevated mental state. What you do before and after brushing may be different according to your purpose, and the actual brushing behavior may be different depending on your purpose as well. I am not recommending one or another of these purposes as preferable to the others. I do suggest, however, that it will benefit you to be clear on which purpose(s) you have in mind while brushing (or any other activity of course).

It takes no deep insight to recognize that the most straightforward purpose among those listed above is the first, that of dental hygiene. And it is worth noting that the second purpose listed is the model purpose for most neurotic behavior; it is aimed primarily at reducing feelings of anxiety. In extension the straightforward purpose can drop from sight altogether while—in neurotic moments—we wash our hands, greet our neighbor, prepare for the party, answer the questions. See what I mean?

Misattention to purpose can result in unnecessary difficulties. An article in *Cosmopolitan* magazine prompted more than 5,500 readers to write asking for additional information about Constructive Living. Their purpose was clear. But not a few letters and cards contained illegible writing, no return address, and somewhat different handwritten addresses on the envelope and in the letter. For whatever reason, the inquiries contained barriers to achieving the simple purpose of receiving details about Constructive Living practice. It was precisely those readers who needed the information most. Purpose needs to guide our action.

DAVID K. REYNOLDS

A LETTER

I wrote this letter to a young lady who entered formal Zen Buddhist training in order to discover the meaning of life and death. She had come close to killing herself in the past. She hoped to find meaning and answers to life by sitting in zazen day after day. But as the years passed, she didn't find any clear answers to the puzzle of life. She spoke to me about her troubles with the feelings that death still called up from the depths of her psyche.

Dear M,

When you realize that the answers to your questions about life and death will never be answered for you (in fact cannot be answered for anyone), please contact me for another approach to your dilemma.

Consideration of death brings with it fear and hope and resignation and peace and a lot of other feelings. It will continue to do so because it does. There is no way or need to change those feelings. Our focus shifts, the feelings change of themselves.

We all learn to live in spite of our knowledge that we shall die someday. Whatever fate has in store for us, the anticipatory anxiety cannot be so disabling that we cannot live fully now. Living fully now (in spite of doubts and fears about the future, in spite of regrets and sorrows from the past) is the only positive prospect for us. And it is wonderfully satisfactory and sufficient. With warm regards.

PUTTING LIFE INTO LIFE

I think it is important that we translated the Japanese words *ikigai ryoho* as "Meaningful *Life* Therapy." It is not Meaningful *Death* Therapy. MLT is not about dying peacefully. It is about living fully until death occurs. The certainty of death forces us to look at how we are living and what we want to accomplish in this time-limited life.

In Constructive Living we have an exercise in which we ask our students to think ahead until the time they might be expected to die and to write their own epitaph (the inscription on the tombstone), obituary (newspaper announcement of death), and eulogy (a speech at the funeral ceremony about the deceased person). Then we cover the student with a sheet and ask some of the following questions:

How old were you when you died?
Who was there with you? What were the ages of your children? Your grandchildren?
Were you alive when your mother/father died? What were their last words to you?
What was most satisfying to you during the last third of your life?
What did you want to do in life but never got around to doing? What prevented your accomplishing some of these important goals?
What specific activities would you have had to change to achieve those unfulfilled goals?
What sorts of property, friends, health, life, hobbies did you have in later life?
Can you give us advice from the grave—to women, men, your children, the elderly, the young?
What was the biggest challenge you faced? What was the most unpleasant event? What was your greatest joy? What was your greatest success?

This exercise is not about dying. It encourages students to think about how they will live the rest of their lives until they die. I think that a serious illness like cancer can encourage people to consider how they will live in much the same way as this exercise does. (See the section of suggested exercises later in this book.)

One of the major contributions of MLT to Japan and to the rest of the world is to create new possibilities of life, new options for suffering humans. Whether a person suffers from cancer or some other life-threatening illness, there is now a choice about responding to the situation. Until Meaningful Life Therapy was founded by Dr. Jinro Itami, it was pretty much assumed in Japan that upon learning of a diagnosis of cancer a patient would give up hope and die rapidly. Now there are many public examples of people who know of their cancer and yet live abundant lives within the physical limitations of their condition. Some individuals have found even more meaning in life after learning of their cancer.

This is a time of creating new roles, new life-styles, new approaches to living. The elderly, too, are creating new ways to grow old actively, meaningfully. When I was a child, most of the elderly women I knew sat all day in rocking chairs grumbling about their health and their inconsiderate children. Now most of the elderly women I know are active, vital participants in society. I am grateful that they have created new possibilities for when I, too, become old—if I live that long.

And so I am grateful to Dr. Itami and those others who have created and developed MLT with their thinking, their hard work, and their lives. Someday I, too, may suffer from some terrible disease. Because of their example I know that illness is not a single path but many paths; and some of the paths travel along high ridges and mountains with a marvelous view.

DOING COURAGE

"Courage is the complement of fear. A man who is fearless cannot be courageous. (He is also a fool.)"
—*Robert Heinlein,* Time Enough for Love

A human without fear is a fool, wrote the late Robert Heinlein, my favorite author of science fiction. Fear complements courage. There is no courage without fear. The members of Meaningful Life Therapy show us their courage by their actions. They do courage. Sometimes they feel fear. It is natural to feel fear in the face of AIDS or any serious illness. Sometimes fear, sometimes courage, sometimes despair, sometimes hope—our feelings change. The stability of life lies in our actions. We can do courage even while afraid.

Some people consider the courageous stories of MLT members to be like the stories of kamikaze pilots, "beyond the limits of human might." Knowing that the cancer may kill them in the end, they continue to hold to MLT purposes (informing other patients, the medical community, and the world of expanded possibilities for living with cancer), which gives their lives special meaning. No longer are they doing courage just for themselves. They do courage for their families, for their society, for humanity. What a wonderful opportunity to make payments on a debt that was contracted even before they were born.

IN CLOSING

In the end Meaningful Life Therapy and Constructive Living are about living. We are all living until we are dead. Let's go about doing that living well.

Theoretical Limits

There are at least two purposes to scientific theories, it seems to me. One is to allow people to investigate the truthfulness of explanations about why things work as they do. The second purpose is to make something look scientific so that scholars and researchers can justify their time and interest in the topic and so that therapists can cite scientific studies in support of their practice. In other words, one purpose is to allow scientific study, and another purpose is to claim scientific respectability.

Most theorizing in the area of psychological counseling isn't aimed at producing testable scientific hypotheses. Most theories of psychotherapy cannot produce testable scientific hypotheses. They do, however, offer intuitive perspectives or orientations toward problems of human living. And they may provide hints about modifications in the practice of psychotherapy to meet the needs of individual clients in a changing world.

But I think we must be wary of getting caught up in words about words about words. Theoretical talk in the area of psychotherapy has the danger of pulling people into philosophical and semantic discussions that stray further and further from grounded, realistic practice. For example, we may be tempted to play word games comparing Constructive Living with a variety of psychotherapy forms and religious practices. If there is to be grounded theory and discussion about reality-based theory in Constructive Living, we must keep asking ourselves the following questions: How is this talk practically contributing to the practice of Constructive Living? How can a student practicing Constructive Living today benefit from this theoretical talk? If we have no answers to these questions, then we would do better spending our time in other areas of our Constructive Living practice than talking about it.

In Japan, Morita therapy—what Morita called experiential therapy—runs the danger of becoming a playground for scholarly chatter. It is now more common to find writings about theory and scholarly research than about its solid roots in personal experience. Morita's words are taken as special truths. Research efforts aim at demonstrating Morita therapy's value and confirming the detailed means by which it works. The fundamental assumptions and theory of Morita therapy itself is unquestioned by nearly all Moritists, though interpretations of theory differ among them.

Few Moritists in Japan appear to reconstruct the truths of this lifeway in their daily experience. It is easier to deal with the method as a therapeutic tool, a conceptual sugar-saline solution, than as an integral part of daily life.

Attachment to Morita's theory, or any theory, can be a useful initial stage, a sort of first-aid measure (along with distraction, waiting for feelings to fade, and use of behavior to influence feelings) during the early periods of unendurable suffering. To believe in an externally devised set of life principles for handling one's distress, to understand a system that explains suffering, to trust an instructor or therapist or guide can provide some temporary relief.

But if one is to press beyond mere temporary surcease from discomfort, one must inevitably develop one's own theory of overcoming neurotic misery based on one's own experience and observation of reality. Put simply, each of us must construct a personal theory, a personal understanding, of distress and growth.

Of course I have some notion of what I believe might be useful as part of your theory. The assignments I recommend to my students aren't randomly devised. Sometimes those assignments are helpful, sometimes not. Each student may discover a set of perceptions, experiences, observations of great personal usefulness. That set won't be the set that Morita discovered or that I discovered. The person who most greatly benefited from Morita's insights was Morita himself. Each of us must do the same if we are to surmount the plateau of dependency on someone else's ideas and experiences.

So if you want theory, you must build it anew from your own experience. If you use Morita's theory or my theory, you are using only words, words that don't spring from the certainty of your own experience. Morita built his theory on his own experience. So did Yoshimoto. So did I.

Don't be caught or hooked or obsessed with anything—not with some theory, not with the word *neurosis,* not even with this very approach to theories presented here.

Morita theory was ailing in Japan because it had become static, without change, mere words. All that was necessary to revive it was to confirm the truth of it for individuals through experience.

Broad Minds

I have never met a mind that didn't judge. That's what minds do—they discriminate, evaluate. Everybody's mind does that. What makes some humans stand out from others is that they don't let their judging minds push their behavior around.

Rather than making efforts to eliminate mental judgments—another of those useless struggles that focus needless attention on natural functions of the mind—simply note the judgments and get on with whatever is more important to be doing. By living constructively we outgrow such narrow-mindedness. Getting caught up in an obsession with perfecting the mind is itself a sort of narrow-mindedness. Such pursuits restrict one's openness to the supporting world, one's attention to what needs doing, one's awareness of new information.

Narrow-minded people don't make broad theories or think grand thoughts. They try to keep their minds under control by means of one-pattern thinking. How dull! The mind should flow naturally and free while their behavior remains under rein.

One of the ways the mind tries to expand is by gathering information. Gathering information seems to be a basic goal of humans.

We travel to get information about others' customs and environments; we watch news on televison; we open the envelopes of ads even when we know we're not going to buy the products; we attend adult-education classes. We are information gatherers and sorters and evaluators. Our minds just aren't satisfied without new information and new problems with which to work.

Something in our minds causes us to search for reality, for truth. We are fascinated by accidents, by disasters—even by those aspects of reality that are disgusting or horrifying. We are drawn to reality even when it is unpleasant and painful—we want to know, for example, when we have cancer or when we are not expected to live much longer. This push to know reality underlies both our search within religion and our research within science. It prompts us to read newspapers and magazines, to watch television and to telephone distant friends.

Even when our sources of information about reality are patently unreliable or untrustworthy or deliberately biased, we still want to know the reality of that false information. How strong is our desire to know about the way things are!

Minds seek challenges too. I sometimes wonder whether the alcohol problem in middle-class and upper-middle-class men and women is less tied to the meaninglessness of life than it is to the ease of life. When life produces few challenges, when daily routine is relatively easily mastered, our minds may generate problems. Can I drink and still carry out my life? Can I get away with this vice without its consuming me? Maybe others can't, but I can meet this challenge. If this hunch has some merit, then it is important to offer alternate stimuli, hurdles, to people with alcohol-abuse problems. The mental exercise involved in living life with full attention may be just what is needed.

It is noteworthy that people with a lot of neurotic moments seem to be obsessed with internally generated information. They focus primarily on distressing data about their own feelings. They notice their feeling-centeredness and then judge or criticize themselves for it. Then they feel even worse. It may take a while for them to realize that feeling is all right, noticing is all right, judging is all right, criticizing is all right, and even feeling worse is all right. What is not all right is letting these natural functions of the mind get in the way of doing the positive, constructive behaviors that will change the focus of their natural minds.

It may be narrow-minded to attempt to construct a life philosophy by thinking on the subject. A life philosophy is the product of one's life, not the other way around. We don't choose a lifeway and then live by it. We grow a life philosophy over years of living one. Excessive rumination about life purpose may be a distraction from what needs doing right before our noses. There is a time for discovering purpose and planning activities, but then there is a time to move on to the next immediate task.

Flip flop goes the lazy mind. People with lazy minds don't recognize the limitations of their minds. Then they encounter some information that tells them they are limited by their thinking. Immediately they turn completely around and think that there are no barriers except in their minds. Similarly, when they discover that they are capable of doing something previously thought impossible, they begin to think they can do anything at all. They think that Constructive Living is either Japanese or it's not. They suspect that Constructive Living must be either psychotherapy or not. They hold that this constructive lifeway is either helpful to everyone or it's not helpful to anyone. In lazy moments our minds try to play either-or games of opposition because to do so is easier than to look at scales of gray percentages. Oversimplification through opposition is a tendency we all need to combat in order to achieve more moments of broad-minded thinking.

People whose broad-minded mental products stand out from those of their peers intrigue us. How amazing is the variety of human mental activity! I sometimes feel an affinity to iconoclasts—to Bankei, the rebel Zen master of the seventeenth century, for example. Iconoclasts don't make themselves. They are just doing their best to describe the world as it looks to them. The eyes of those around them produce iconoclasts.

DAVID K. REYNOLDS

Reading can provide a mind-broadening exercise. For example, science fiction can be important by allowing us to see humanity from a distance or from an alien or universal point of view. It is not we Americans or we Japanese but we humans, we inhabitants of this planet. Well-written science fiction stretches and broadens the mind.

Feelings Are for Feeling

You won't see me cry in public. It's not that I'm cold and insensitive. It's not that I'm suppressing feelings or ignoring them or pretending I'm not feeling what I am. I have a choice whether to let others in on what I'm feeling; mostly I choose not to do so. When I cry, I'd prefer to be alone.

Some men these days are being criticized by factions of women and other men for not being expressive of their emotions. Those criticisms are based on unrealistic assumptions. Here are a few of them:

Critics assume that the only two possibilities for handling feelings are to express them or to suppress them. The third alternative—recognizing them, acknowledging them without external expression, and getting on with doing what needs doing—isn't considered, although that third alternative is the one we all utilize most of the time.

Critics don't seem to realize that both sexes hold back expression of feelings most of the time. We cannot be bothered with expressing every feeling that pops up in our psyches, nor do others wish to be bothered with an ongoing report of our fluctuating mood state. It would be a burden on others to have to put up with a stream of messages about our feelings. We all hide our feelings, if you will.

If you look closely at the complaints about nonexpression of feelings by males, you will see that the critics call for the increased expression of only *certain kinds* of feelings in certain circumstances. Anger, sorrow, vulnerability, and the like are primarily targeted. I have never understood why these particular feelings should be displayed for others on demand. I suspect that the attempt to coerce males into expressing these feelings in social contexts is an attempt at some sort of social leveling, a distorted effort by the critics to get some social confirmation of their own feelings. But feeling any feeling is all right. We don't need to be reassured that others have these feelings too. They do.

I continue to be intrigued that people believe they have secret feelings known only to mental health professionals who are capable of putting their clients in touch with those feelings. That belief is not so different from believing that we are unwittingly possessed by devils that can be exorcised by some religious professionals. Interestingly, the feelings that we are supposed to have lurking in our psyches are uniformly unpleasant ones. Why can't we get in touch with our hidden joy? Why can't we discover we've been happy all these years without knowing it? Sounds sort of foolish, doesn't it? If such a psychotherapy doesn't exist already, it is on its way.

With rare exceptions Western psychology doesn't value individual experience while claiming that it does. What it values is *interpreted* individual experience. The interpretation must be provided by or at least validated by the professional. Rather than acknowledging the full implications of feelings, for example, much of Western psychological counseling seems to trivialize and discount feelings. When feelings are considered to be merely markers of past parental mistakes or signs of current psychological diagnostic categories or indications of the working of the unconscious (or other mystical, untestable constructions), then the feelings themselves are primarily tokens of "more important" phenomena. It is important to recognize the value of the experienced feeling and the information it brings. When one is engaged in fighting the feeling or "curing" its cause, the focus remains on escape; in order to derive full benefit from a feeling it must be accepted, incorporated into momentary life experience, not resisted.

It increasingly appears that much of Western psychological counseling aims at little more than distraction from genuine and natural emotions through specialized cognitive maneuvering. It is time that we stopped trying to "fix" feelings and got on with the more important and practical objective of feeling feelings and learning from them while engaging in purposeful behavior.

Someday we'll learn that feelings—any and all feelings—are for feeling.

Creativity

What has Constructive Living to say about creativity? Is it a neglected area of Constructive Living thought?

As always, when little is known about a subject, Constructive Living theorists readily recognize our lack of knowledge. If anyone knew the sources and stimuli for creativity, we would encourage their development. There are, however, competing theories on the subject, none of which is convincing to me.

Creative thoughts, like any thoughts, come from nowhere or some "unknownwhere" and flash into my mind. They are gifts from reality, if you like.

My responsibility is to give those creative thoughts time and opportunity to arise and to record them so that they aren't lost. A certain amount of mental stimulation seems helpful for me, as well as a certain amount of quiet time alone. Reading, conversations, television, films, watercolors, and so forth stimulate my thinking. Isolated walks in the woods, garden work, and standing in front of this word processor help me sift these ideas.

Sometimes the ideas come, and sometimes they don't. What is controllable is my recording of the ideas when they do emerge. If I fail to note them down, they may be lost, unavailable for kneading or rising or the baking of these rough loaves. If I fail to make them publicly available through writing and speaking, then I betray this creativity. It is my loss; reality has other channels of communication.

There is a theme in Constructive Living that in the doing of a task (any purposeful action) new richness occurs. Not only in the thinking about doing or the planning to do are we informed, but in the doing itself experiential lessons are learned. Writing fits this theme. As I do the physical acts of pressing fingers against the keys of this keyboard, further thoughts emerge. To call these thoughts mine seems arrogant and foolish. To call my effort at recording them mine seems more sensible (the action aspect of CL) and equally foolish (the reflection aspect of CL). To work on stimulating "my" creativity appears to be as strange an undertaking as trying to fathom it. Straightforward receptivity and acceptance of what reality sends seems more reasonable . . . acting, all the while, to influence that reality.

What about lofty and creative dreams? CL seems so down to earth, so immediate and practical, that perhaps it may be misinterpreted as ignoring such domains. Humans need distant and fantastic goals too. Yet if such dreams are to be anything more than escapist imaginings, there must be smaller goals and actions on the way to achieving and sustaining the larger purposes.

America has always been a country of great dreams. What has slipped away from many is the effort of work and the willingness to wait in order to make the dreams real. There is no lack of distant dreams and models—movie stars, singers, athletes, novelists, figures of wealth and power. Few seem to see that the bigger the dream, the more effort is required in many small actions over the long run to increase the likelihood of success. Creative ideas and grand dreams are fairly common; actualizing them is much less common.

DAVID K. REYNOLDS

The Perfect Mate

◀◀◉▶▶

There is nothing wrong with going for the best, unless perfectionism and ideals interfere with doing our realistic best right now. Professor Akira Ishii tells the story of his disappointing experience with eels. When he was a child, he loved to eat broiled eels, but they are a delicacy in Japan and rather expensive. So he never got his fill of eels. Then on his eleventh or twelfth birthday his family treated him to all the eels he could eat. How wonderful! He ate his fill. But thereafter he compared the few skimpy eels served to him in restaurants with the feast he had eaten as a youth. How disappointing! Then one evening he was served eels that were so delicious, they made him forget how few there were. Unfortunately after that meal he kept comparing the flavor of the eels served to him in ordinary restaurants with those tasty eels of the past. Again he was disappointed. At last he came to realize that the eel on the plate right in front of him was the best eel in the world. The disappointment generated by perfectionistic comparison disappeared.

Not a few people who come to me are disappointed with their partners. Husbands, wives, lovers, business associates, boyfriends, girlfriends, same sex or not—they all seem to be imperfect. They fail to live up to our ideals. The partner may not offer enough intellectual stimulation or passion or determination to succeed. It is noteworthy that the very trait the partner lacks becomes the most important trait possible. The positive qualities are taken for granted while the negative qualities draw attention and concern. Of course we may have some minor imperfections, too, but at least we are working on them. Those partners don't seem to care about self-improvement.

As you know, Constructive Living never recommends ignoring reality. I would never suggest that you lie to yourself about your partner, that you pretend your partner is perfect. However, focusing only on faults is a kind of ignoring of reality too. We don't usually find ourselves in partnerships with people who have no endearing qualities. Something attracted us to them initially. That eel in front of you is the best eel in the world for you right now. Even if you are working toward a divorce or separation or breaking the partnership, you will find it useful to find positive qualities and to thank and praise your partner for those qualities. Yes, even while doing what needs to be done to dissolve the partnership. To do so is not hypocrisy, it is recognizing and acknowledging a part of reality you may have noticed right along or forgotten.

Life is uncertain. People come and go. When we find someone who has many of the attributes we hope for in a partner, we may latch on to that person and wish he or she had those few missing qualities. We may try to get everything we need from one person. But trying to fill even our social needs in one partner may be impossible. Relatives, friends, acquaintances, neighbors, memberships, sporting companions, and the like may be necessary.

But in addition to these real social needs is a need for a reasonable attitude toward others. When my life is geared primarily toward getting my social (or any other personal) needs met, there will always be dissatisfaction. When my attitude is truly geared toward seeing that my partner's (friend's, neighbor's) actions are being appreciated and his or her needs are being met, then there is a real chance for satisfaction. Remember, the best way to meet others' needs is not to be their obedient slave. That is mere cowardice and laziness. Finding the dignified, honorable, practical,

DAVID K. REYNOLDS

sensible way to appreciate and serve others is a difficult and rewarding undertaking.

Again, when the emphasis is on getting my share, I'll always be disappointed. When the emphasis is on realistically recognizing what I am already receiving and on working to repay those around me, this is the only genuine opportunity for fulfillment. Taking care of me first *includes* taking care of others. The two objectives aren't separate and they certainly can't be done effectively in some serial order, one after another.

I Alone Suffer

There is a common myth that no one suffers as we do and that no one else can understand our suffering. Each of my beginning students is likely to believe that he or she suffers uniquely and alone and more than other people.

Rev. Shue Usami, head of Senkobo Temple in Mie Prefecture, tells about a man who complained to his doctor, "I suffer so much from this operation." His doctor's reply was, "Yes, we all suffer from your operation—your family, your nurses, and I do too." The patient considered only his own distress. The doctor reminded him that others shared distress too. His family was worried and inconvenienced by their visits to the hospital; the doctor had to stay up the night after the operation to watch his patient's progress; the nurses were called upon for extra vigilance and special care. It is rare to suffer alone. The wavelets of our misery extend to other people.

Whether my students are challenging cancer or fears of leaving the house, whether they struggle with torturing memories or abusive spouses, they benefit from being able to see the interlocking circles of shared suffering of which they are a part. As always, the primary benefit is straightforwardly seeing more of reality, the way things are. That realistic view is in itself vital for our mental health. In addition, the recognition that we don't hurt alone can bring some measure of relief from feelings of isolation and alienation. Furthermore, concern with others' suffering and our attempts to alleviate it offer an opportunity for selfless action that distracts us from self-focused misery.

Some people seem to build their social identity on their degree of suffering. Their "claim to fame" rests on tragedy after tragedy. They are like children who compare the scabs and scrapes on their knees to see who has the worst. We all have scrapes on our knees. Scrapes, too, are nothing special.

How can we prepare ourselves and our students for the occasional inevitable failure? Life brings us all sorts of challenges; sometimes we rise to the occasion, sometimes not. When a student fails to complete an assignment, there may be self-recrimination and reverberations of past failures and inadequacy. The Constructive Living position on missed assignments is the same as that of any other situation; What needs to be done now? Reality just keeps coming.

We can respond to a mistake with the emotion-laden reaction "Oh, no! Failed again!" or we can respond with attention to the nature of the new situation presented by our mistake and what needs to be done about it. In general we work to replace the domination of a feeling response with a reasonable-action response. The feeling response doesn't disappear altogether, but it is no longer the primary focus of our attention.

Failure, suffering, dilemmas, crises—all are part of human existence. They are not the whole of it. Our understanding of them and our response to them lie within our control. What needs doing next?

I used to think that some people were born with common sense and some were born without it. Now I know that common sense is earned by many experiences and many failures.

Identity's Iron Lace

Constructive Living highlights my own actions. It is about my doing what needs to be done. When I get distracted by trying to get others to do what I have decided they need to do, there is trouble. It is unwise to shift the fulcrum of personal freedom into the bog of uncontrollability.

There is a solid independence to people who walk the Constructive Living path. We have different levels of skill in social situations. But even when cooperating with others in some joint project, even when intimately involved with a beloved partner, there is a recognition of our inherent autonomy. That singularity is not a matter of personal style, I suspect, but a fundamental perspective fostered by Constructive Living. Reality keeps telling us that we do and die alone, no matter how many people are nearby. Perhaps for some that recognition of independence seems to prompt feelings of loneliness and isolation. But it need not. It is just the way things are. It is as indicative of freedom and possibility as it is of confinement and limits.

Furthermore, it defines life's game in terms of rules that allow each of us to win no matter what the other players are doing. Even when your spouse or boss or co-worker has an off moment, you don't have to lose that moment's game. Similarly they have the potential to win each moment of their life games even when you are not functioning at top form. Seen in this light, Constructive Living views life more like tennis singles or golf than like football or baseball.

Having emphasized this independence of responsibility and action, I must also acknowledge the influence of others on our lives. Read a book, counsel a student, share a home with someone—we take on some of the characteristics of the characters with whom we interact. Without necessarily wanting to or realizing it, we can't resist their influence. So it is very important to select carefully those with whom we spend time. We shall become like them (and they shall become like us). It is helpful to ask ourselves questions like Do I want to become more like the characters in this author's books? Do I want to be more like the characters in this television program or film or play? Do I genuinely want to resemble this man or woman (and his parents and friends and children—for they, too, are in the spheres of influence surrounding that person)?

Preserving or generating a positive identity, a good self-image, is a key element in recent Western psychotherapies and self-growth techniques. Pride is touted as the cure-all for psychological and social problems. Don't believe it. Loving action will do more to solve such problems than pride.

Pride is about receiving and self-protection, about one's own fair share. Loving action is about giving and supporting, about the loved one's share and more. Some people will tell you that you must have the pride, the self-love first in order to do the loving action for others. Don't buy such talk. They are selling self-love, a readily marketable product. Unfortunately such people don't know how to generate anything beyond a shadowy assertive self-centeredness. *Pride in oneself* is a pale cousin to the much more solid *confidence in reality*. But if you seek self-love, you are more likely to find it in intelligently giving yourself away in loving action than in "working on yourself."

Giving yourself away out of habit or timidity is merely inefficient and exhausting. Take some time to consider what those around you really need from you, then offer it. The goal is not its effects on you but their benefit. Then see what your loving action does for your identity. For all our aspirations and affirmations, we are what we do.

DAVID K. REYNOLDS

Construction and Living

I'm in the process of putting small sleeping rooms in an unfinished basement. My carpentry skills up until now were pretty much limited to assembling ready-made furniture and installing wall paneling. Until last week I couldn't have identified a two-by-four or a four-by-six on sight. I didn't know what a joist hanger was or a shim. I may once have known, but had forgotten that nails are bought by the pound. Simple things. Fortunately Ron Madson, a Constructive Living carpenter these days, drove up from San Francisco to offer some experienced advice on practical details of the project.

Now I'm often happily (if not skillfully) measuring, sawing, and pounding away. Already I've learned that planning and forethought can save trips back and forth to the lumber supplier, can avoid some redoing of tasks, can simplify the work somewhat. Of course I learned these lessons by failing to do the proper planning and thinking; I learned them the hard way. That's all right. Reality teaches.

I'm learning to keep my tools in predictable places so that I don't spend lots of time searching for them. I'm learning to visualize the structure so that work proceeds in the proper order. A flying chip of wood reminded me to wear those safety goggles. The lessons are there when I am alert to them.

It is fine to be a beginner, even a fool. We can't be proficient at everything, especially at first. Experience gives us a shot at competency. Daydreams don't.

Causes

There was a time in academic and clinical psychology when people believed that schizophrenia was caused by improper parenting. There was a belief that certain kinds of interactions between parent and child (the "double-bind" theory, for example) could cause the child to withdraw from reality and become psychotic. During this period parents of schizophrenic children were likely to feel guilt at having caused their child's problem. After a time, researchers began to realize that quite normal parents of children who would become schizophrenic were having trouble interacting normally with their disturbed children. It may have been that the parents initiated some unhealthy interactions with the children, but the children caused some of the unhealthy interactions too. Attention shifted from exclusive focus on the faults of the parents to some genetic disorder of the child that preceded the child-rearing problems and contributed to the difficulties between parents and children somehow. I suspect that most researchers these days see schizophrenia as the result of a combination of some genetic biochemical susceptibility along with triggering and sustaining life experiences.

There is a parallel here to the fashion of thinking about neurotic life problems these days. It is very fashionable to consider childhood abuse and neglect as *the* cause of all sorts of adult problems. Parental alcoholism, physical and sexual and verbal abuse, and the like are considered the primary causes of everything from headaches and shyness to multiple personalities and substance abuse. Life is not so simple. Parents are not so easily blamed. Although it is convenient for adult children to place accountability on parents' shoulders, it is an oversimplification, just as it was in schizophrenia studies forty years ago. We shall outgrow this fad. We shall come to recognize that children contributed to their own troubled childhoods and caused trouble for their parents, as well as the reverse. Moreover, we shall come to see that the oversimplified paper doll images of abusive parents were only part of the picture. Those same deficient parents also provided shelter, work, interest, encouragement, and other material and nonmaterial benefits to their children. I am not denying that our parents were imperfect. They were. So are we. I am suggesting that it is about time to give up the childish notion that parents were the "bad guys" and get on with responsible living now.

A Coos Bay, Oregon, teacher holds a six-year-old boy's candy bar while he eats lunch; she promises to return the treat after school. "If my blood sugar gets too low and I punch somebody out it's your fault," he tells her. This first-grade child has learned that low blood sugar may be considered by some to be a cause of (read here "excuse for") hitting another child. Such thinking is not only misguided, it is dangerous. If society is to survive and progress we must emphasize personal responsibility for behavior and avoid teaching sophisticated but mistaken strategies for avoiding responsibility. Beware that tempting path toward social chaos.

Extenuating emotional circumstances have been accepted as a defense plea in a great many criminal trials. I sometimes have trouble understanding the meaning of "out of control." When a murderer asserts that he couldn't control his behavior it doesn't mean that his arms and legs twitched out of control. He carefully drove the car, opened the door, pulled the trigger. That looks like control of behavior to me. Are emotions thought to cause us to lose control

DAVID K. REYNOLDS

of only certain behaviors? How convenient for lawyers and therapists.

Personality is thought to cause behavior, too. Certainly we can find a certain degree of regularity in individuals' behavior. We may choose to call that regularity of behavior "personality." But then we may not cite "personality" as the *cause* of regularity of behavior. To do so would create a circular argument. So it means nothing to talk about working on or improving personality in order to correct behavior. The two processes, if they mean anything at all, are the same.

It is rather like calling the regularity of ups and downs in the Pacific Ocean "tides" and then explaining the rising and falling of the ocean with the term *tides*. But tides don't cause the rising and falling of the Pacific Ocean. Something else does—the moon's gravitational pull is the cause. Frankly, I am not sure what causes behavior. I seriously doubt that anyone else is either, though there is no lack of psychological theories concerned with the matter.

I have written these words before: No one has any idea why anyone does anything. All our talk about causes is talk. All our fancy psychodynamic theories are as ephemeral as smoke. Our ability to explain, or predict, individual behavior in natural circumstances with regularity is effectively nil. People are complex and changing. Circumstances are complex and changing. We just don't know.

So it is better to get on with doing what we know needs doing. Let's abandon the complex, misty rationales. I did what I did. Now what needs doing?

Setting the Date

Do you think you may need to make a change in your life? Perhaps it's your partner, your job, your house, your car, a habitual behavior. The problem has been bothering you in a mild way, but not to the degree that you've done anything to alter the situation. Perhaps the situation doesn't need to be changed at all. Changing does involve time and effort. And what will your life be like afterward? Would all the effort be worth it?

Such thinking is pretty common, I suspect. The default result of just vaguely considering a change is that the status quo remains. An alternative to idle speculation and low-grade discomfort is to set a date for change. It is easier to set a date that is off in the future, say, six months or a year. The default action now signifies change. But, at the start, the change is safely distant in time.

Communicating the date to others and displaying it in a conspicuous place are good ideas. These behaviors reinforce your commitment and mobilize others to assist or resist or at least consider what you are planning to do. Within a reasonable period of time prior to the change date you should be making specific, detailed plans. Preferably, the plans should be written. You may wish to get input from others about these exact plans. Again, the very effort of asking for feedback from others reinforces your social commitment to following through on your movement.

Sometimes, as the change date approaches, new circumstances arise that affect your decision. Your partner may make major revisions or housing values may go down or you may get a promotion. If the target date no longer seems appropriate, it may be useful to reset the date back another six months or a year or so. Resetting the date is usually a better strategy than abandoning it altogether. There was some reason why you set the date in the first place.

At last the time has come to make the change. How do you get yourself to do it? Perhaps you know by now that there is no magical way to make difficult actions easy. No exploration or affirmation or imagination, no resolve or determination or decision is necessary. Just do it. Keep your attention on the shifts in your environment that result from your changing. Keep your awareness open for what needs doing. Move on to what needs doing next.

Give the new circumstances a chance. It's pretty common for there to be rough edges and discomfort during a period of change. Don't immediately rush back into the security of old familiar unpleasantness. Set a future date for another change, if necessary. And get on with your life.

Too Soft

Some readers will take this chapter as just the musing of a hard-line theorist and so will be able to dismiss it. Others will see it as another attempt to chop away at your roots just as you begin to feel comfortable—a sort of existential, Zen-like tactic aimed, perhaps, at freeing humans from any orthodoxy. Take it as you will; I suspect we need to rethink the idea of a soft-line and hard-line approach to Constructive Living.

THE DISTINCTION

In the hard-line approach to the action aspect of Constructive Living, the instructor makes no genuine attempt to explain or interpret the students' difficulties. The students' personal experiences while completing (or not completing) the assignments will provide the necessary understanding. No one really knows why we do what we do. Reality is the teacher. Explanations are superfluous misdirections. Just do it.

In the soft-line approach the instructor makes efforts to provide explanations and interpretations, which are intended to encourage the student to complete the assignments. The student is given more time to discuss issues of emotion.

In the soft-line approach to the reflection aspect of Constructive Living, the students are encouraged to see the positive contributions of others in their lives. Those who were thought to be villains may take on heroic aspects. Parents may be more appreciated than before. The students discover a deeper sense of having been loved over the years. Understandably this approach is more attractive than the aspect of reality that the hard line emphasizes.

In the hard-line approach students are encouraged to see their own failure to give to others who cared for them. Rather than seeing themselves as heroes who overcame the limitations of improper childrearing and a hostile fate, they begin to see themselves as selfish takers concerned primarily with getting their share and more from the world. The prospect of seeing this reality isn't pleasant.

Of course most Constructive Living instructors shift back and forth between the soft line and hard line when confronted with the ups and downs of a student's progress. It does little good to alienate a student with a rigidly hard-line delivery, particularly during the first few sessions. However, the student's strength and independence cannot be developed, and the depths of Constructive Living cannot be plumbed, with a soft-line approach alone.

THE PROBLEM

I'm beginning to doubt the wisdom of introducing in *A Thousand Waves* the hard-line—soft-line distinction in the action or Morita element of Constructive Living. It seems to give the mistaken impression that soft Constructive Living is a sort of psychotherapy. It isn't. At an advanced training conference a few years ago several psychotherapists with Constructive Living training began to speak with great authority about the doing of Constructive Living instruction during a role-playing session. They were giving advice on the basis of their experience with psychotherapy, having misinterpreted Constructive Living to be a kind of Japanese psychotherapy.

The soft-line notion seems to hold the danger of permitting

instructors to misperceive Constructive Living as merely another style of Western psychotherapy or counseling. It is not psychotherapy but reeducation, as Morita put it. It is something so radically and vitally different from psychotherapy that Morita could call his method a Copernican Revolution. Constructive Living has plenty of room for individual style, but the soft-line notion seems to have opened the door for all sorts of concerns and methods that are unrelated or antithetical to its core.

During certification training each trainee meets with me for individual sessions. I model the Constructive Living approach during those sessions. I ask if they are eating, sleeping, exercising well. What are their assignments? What have they been noticing? What needs doing? The sessions don't resemble traditional Western psychotherapy sessions. On purpose.

In the introduction to this book I offered advice to mental health professionals. Here is some related advice to nonprofessionals: Beware of good-hearted and well-intentioned efforts by mental health professionals to make Constructive Living instructors with little experience into amateur psychotherapists with even less experience. Don't be intimidated by professional degrees, licenses, and other credentials. The training of a mental health professional typically offers useful experiences and interpersonal skills. It does not confer wisdom or (sometimes) even reality-based knowledge. It may, in fact, hinder the understanding of Constructive Living.

DAVID K. REYNOLDS

Guided-Reflection Experience

━━━━━━━━━ ◄◄◖●◗►► ━━━━━━━━━

[This exercise is adapted, with appreciation, from Akira Ishii's method of introducing Naikan reflection to groups.]

We'll begin with reflection on your mother during kindergarten and the first grade. The three themes for reflection in this case are:

- What did you receive from your mother during this period?
- What did you return to your mother during this period?
- What troubles did you cause your mother during this period?

SETTING THE STAGE

Please close your eyes and find a comfortable sitting position. Think back to the house you lived in during kindergarten and the first grade. If there was more than one house, consider the one you remember most clearly. Where did you play? Remember your yard, a nearby park, the neighborhood streets.

Think back to your room, the place where you slept. Recall the dresser, the light, your bed, your toys. Recall the kitchen, the bathroom of the house, the garage.

What did your mother (or the person who had primary responsibility for your care) do for you? Reflect on your meals. What were your favorite foods? Who served you seconds when you wanted more? Did you have a special dish or cup at mealtime? Were there special foods prepared at holidays, at your birthday?

Who washed your body? Your hair? Who wiped the soap from your eyes? Who dried off your small body? Can you remember a particular time when your mother did something special for you? Did she go with you to school on your first day? Who buttoned and zipped your clothing that day? Who combed or braided your hair? Who wrote your name on your clothing and made lunch for you? Who woke you up each morning and sent you off to school? Who warmed your room for your return? Who had a snack waiting for you? Did she help you with homework, with projects from Brownies or Cub Scouts? Perhaps she laid out your clothes after a bath, changed the sheets on your bed, laundered clothes muddied from playing or wet from snow.

When you were sick, who cared for you? Did she sit by your bed and put cool cloths on your hot forehead? Did she measure out the medicine while you complained of its bitter taste? Who fluffed your pillow? Who transported you to the doctor's office? To the hospital?

Who selected your clothing? Your birthday and holiday presents? Did she do the shopping for those special occasions? Who helped you open packages that were too difficult for your small hands and strength?

WHAT DID YOU DO FOR HER?

What did you do for your mother during those days? Did you help her carry groceries? Do dishes? Clean house? Can you think of anything you did for her that didn't indirectly benefit you? After all, you, too, ate the groceries and you, too, ate from the dishes you washed. How about a present for her on her birthday or for

Mother's Day? Did you make it? Buy it? With whose materials? With whose money? You may find it difficult to come up with recollections of things you returned to your mother.

WHAT TROUBLES DID YOU CAUSE HER?

How about troubles you caused her? Perhaps you played after dark and caused her to worry about you. Perhaps you wet your bed and woke her in the night wanting to sleep with her when she was tired from the day's work.

On the days you didn't want to go to school, what was the effect on your mother? How about when you fought with other kids and got hurt? Was she troubled when you refused to eat foods you disliked, when you cried in stores wanting the toys you saw on the shelves? Can you recall some of these specific events?

CONCLUDING THOUGHTS

Let's take a few minutes to let your mind roam freely during this period in your past. Can you come up with something else received from your mother, something returned to her, some trouble caused her?

Now open your eyes.

It may be difficult to remember details at first. However, if you allow yourself thirty minutes or so each time, you may be surprised at the extent to which you are able to recall new details with each attempt at retrospection. We know from solid scientific research that the memories are coded in the brain and can be elicited by means of electrical stimulation with electrodes. But we can learn to access the memories without complicated electrical apparatus, just by practicing.

There may be unpleasant memories welling up too. Memories you wish would stay forgotten. But they, too, are part of the reality of your past. And the more you do this guided reminiscence, the more you will find the unpleasant memories overshadowed by the vast numbers of services and things received in spite of your imperfection, in spite of the fact that you didn't recognize at the time that you were receiving, in spite of your lack of gratitude or repayment. The pressure is off; we no longer need to try to attain perfection in the eyes of others to receive their support—we have been receiving their support all along, flawed though we are. What a relief to realize this truth—not just once, intellectually, but over and over again through the cumulative effect of recalling specific concrete events from the past. We are no longer bound by our past experiences. Instead we are freed by looking at them carefully, in detail.

I recommend that you repeat this reflection of your mother during other periods of your life. You might want to consider the grammar school years, junior high school years, senior high school years, and so on in three-year periods up to the present or until your mother died. Then you might begin again with your earliest childhood years reflecting on your father or the male most like a father to you. Repeat the process for three-year periods up to the present or until your father died. Then try reflecting on other family members and relatives, on teachers, friends, spouse, anyone who has influenced your life. This is the intensive-reflection aspect of Constructive Living; it is called Naikan.

Deliberations on Reflection in Constructive Living

We make a living by what we get. We make a life by what we give.
—Winston Churchill

The reflection aspect of Constructive Living is based on a reflective practice called Naikan, meaning "inner observation" or "looking within" in Japanese. The fundamental Naikan practice is quite simple and straightforward. It involves examining our memories of ourselves and others in our lives. One by one we look at what we received from others at particular times in our past, what we gave to them in return, and the troubles we caused them during those periods. Naikan invites us to take a realistic look at the past, one that isn't colored by our usual attempts to make ourselves appear to be heroes who have struggled to overcome immense obstacles and have achieved our success thanks to our own efforts alone.

A number of related Constructive Living practices have been developed with Naikan-like themes. We assign exercises such as saying thank you at least ten times a day, writing letters of apology to those we have wronged in the past, volunteering to clean up beaches and parks, doing secret services for others, and the like.

The rest of this chapter contains observations inspired by the reflection aspect of Constructive Living.

1. ANOTHER PERSPECTIVE

Consumer values assume that one's money is one's own. I have the right to spend my money as I please, wisely and efficiently or foolishly. However, the reflection aspect of Constructive Living suggests that the money I consider my own is not wholly mine. What I call "my" money is "mine" thanks to the efforts of those who hired me, and paid me, and bought the products I produce, and kept my car running so that I could get to work, and fed me so that I had energy to work, and constructed my office building and the tools of my trade, and so on. My earnings are the result of a cooperative venture, whether I choose to recognize it or not. My checking account is in my name, but I am merely a sort of steward of it.

Christians and Jews should not find such a perspective strange. The Judeo-Christian tradition holds us accountable as stewards of the bounty that comes from God. Religious tradition might consider this reflection to be a method of specifying the detailed means by which that bounty is delivered.

Even the talk of alternative belief systems about a reified Earth Mother and Sea Mother becomes more understandable when seen through the lens of CL reflection. The concept of a Sea Mother may appear quite mystical if we reify the symbol and forget its basis in concrete reality. The sea does keep producing fish and other delights for us and turns them over to us freely. Our mothers, too, prepared our meals when we were children and offered the food freely to us. CL asks us to look at the concrete, detailed reality (the only way reality comes to us, after all) that prompted the creation of these images.

2. HIDDEN MEMORIES

The mind brings up past emotion-laden events again and again. Some theories suggest that to do so leaches some of the emotional tone from the memory. Time serves that function. I suspect the recollection restimulates feelings associated with the event rather than milking the memories of feeling. The real value in bringing up such events is in having the opportunity to rethink or reinterpret what happened and to reconsider what appropriate goals and actions were present. Both the action and the reflection aspects of CL are useful here.

It appears from our experience with CL reflection that memories can be stored away for decades and accessed much later. The memories seem to have associated feelings. Furthermore the memories are coded in such detail as to be capable of being evaluated by the three reflection themes of what was received from others, what was returned to others, and what troubles were caused others, as we have seen.

Electrical stimulation of the cortex of the brain provides some evidence that such elaborate memory storage is possible. For example, the following two quotations rely on classic cortical-stimulation research:

> [Memories'] extraordinary and consistent detail, which was evoked each time the cortex was stimulated, and exceeded anything which could be recalled by ordinary memory, suggested to Penfield that the brain retained an almost perfect record of every lifetime's experience, that the total stream of consciousness was preserved in the brain, and, as such, could always be evoked or called forth, whether by the ordinary needs and circumstances of life, or by the extraordinary circumstances of an epileptic or electrical stimulation [pp. 137–138, from The Man Who Mistook His Wife for a Hat, by Oliver Sacks, 1970].

> We surmise that our patient (like everybody) is stacked with an almost infinite number of "dormant" memory-traces, some of

which can be reactivated under special conditions, especially conditions of overwhelming excitement. Such traces, we conceive—like the subcortical imprints of remote events far below the horizon of mental life—are indelibly etched in the nervous system, and may persist indefinitely in a state of abeyance, due either to lack of excitation or to positive inhibition. . . . All of these states can "release" memory, and all of them can lead to a re-experience and re-enactment of the past [Ibid. p. 152].

This notion of stored memories and feelings is quite different from the undemonstrated hypothesis that feelings continue to percolate in some unconscious area of the mind until they are expressed and thus exorcised. Research evidence indicates that the memory of a feeling is probably stored throughout one's lifetime, whether the feeling is expressed or not.

3. ABSURDITIES

I sometimes assign as homework the task of writing a letter of apology to a significant other from the past. There is an assortment of ways to sabotage such a letter. Students may have difficulty recalling having done anything worthy of apology; they may only remember the other party's actions that hurt them. One young lady began her letter with "I'm sorry for that thing you seem to think I did to you."

In my lectures about Constructive Living I usually include material about stages of development resulting from the action and reflection aspects of CL. I invariably point out that even those who master this or other enlightening lifeways aren't free from occasional misery. During the questioning period following a lecture one intense young man wanted to know whether he had correctly understood what I said.

"You mean that even enlightened people aren't free from misery?" he asked.

DAVID K. REYNOLDS

"Yes, that's exactly what I mean," I replied.

"Oh, God!" The exclamation jumped from his lips with such spontaneity that everyone laughed. Another illusion shattered.

Humans have a devious side. Too many of us search so desperately for some excuse for avoiding responsibility in our lives that we probe for childhood abuse even when it existed in only its most innocuous forms, and we ignore the countless acts of diaper changing and meal preparation and rides to music lessons, more than one of which clearly existed in our past. For the vast majority of us our parents demonstrated "doing-love" even when we were unlovable as children. How easy it is to dismiss the effort Mother put into shopping and selecting and paying for my sweater by emphasizing that the sweater didn't fit my preferences for style and color.

A final note about absurdity. Akira Ishii points out that the person with a grudge doesn't sleep well, gnashing his teeth, but the person who is the target of the grudge, not knowing about it, sleeps perfectly well. The one with the grudge is suffering. This guided reflection helps relieve some of that unnecessary suffering.

4. CONTRIBUTIONS

One fairly common problem my students bring to our teaching sessions involves some decision they must make in their lives. They have considered the pros and cons of their problem, weighing a spectrum of factors. But the scales appear evenly balanced—to move or not to move, to accept the promotion or to decline it, to continue in the partnership or to dissolve it, to purchase the house or to continue renting, to use the cash windfall for education or for travel.

One contribution the reflective aspect of Constructive Living can make toward resolution of this sort of dilemma is to add a new set of criteria for deciding. Ordinarily the students have pretty much considered their own desires and convenience in relation to the decision. But what about the effects of their decision on others?

Naikan flips the primary criterion from what would work out best for me to what would work out best for others, even if I were inconvenienced. Now, why on earth should anyone consider a decision from that perspective?

Another contribution involves providing a life game with the possibility of winning all the time. If my goal is to make sure I secure my share of life's bounty, then I'll sometimes win and sometimes lose at life's game. However, if my goal is to work on repaying my debt to reality's representatives around me, the possibility of continuous success lies within my grasp. Winning can lie outside or within my control depending on how life's game is scored.

Of course in the long run I cannot win the contest between giving and receiving in life. With my competitive spirit I would like to have a shot at giving to the world more than I receive. But when I look carefully, the gifts from reality are always greater than what I give. Perhaps if I go hiking alone in nature, I won't be taking so much from other humans, I thought. But I walked on trails made by others wearing shoes made by people I never met. My energy came from food prepared by hands other than my own and worked through a body given to me by my parents. The debt is inescapable.

But whatever the other benefits of these recollections within the practice of Constructive Living, the major benefit is that they lead us to attend to and respond to reality. Being realistic in the best sense of the word is the main goal of Constructive Living. Being realistic offers us the greatest opportunity for developing a balanced life. As Gregory Willms, a Constructive Living instructor in Santa Rosa, California, points out, Constructive Living offers a combination of reflection and action in some ways like the balanced life of contemplation and action in medieval Europe.

5. WARMTH

The winter chill of the Oregon coast energizes me. It also leads me to notice and appreciate heat. When I remove warm pajamas or a warm sweater, I can feel the stored heat in the garment. It moves away from my body almost reluctantly. More of my attention these days turns to considerations of heat. What clothes shall I wear? How much insulation does the basement need? Are the water pipes properly shielded? Shall I heat the water served at lunch? How sluggish my fingers are at the computer keyboard this chilly morning! Has the cold caused the error messages at startup of this computer? Is there sufficient wood in for the winter? Are the road conditions icy?

Having spent most of my childhood and adult years in southern California and Hawaii, I took my friend, heat, for granted. It was even an annoying guest at times, one who prompted me to think in terms of avoidance. At worst it could be ignored and endured like a repetitious television commercial. But we have grown closer recently, heat and I. I am learning to appreciate its finer points.

Do these words sound strange? Does it seem odd to anthropomorphize or personalize heat in this way? Is it merely some sort of literary flirtation? Consider the following reasoning. One of the ways we can discover the nature of our involvement with heat and vacuum cleaners and pens and eating utensils and telephones, as well as with people, is by looking at the specific details of everyday reality. If I say to myself, "How pleasant heat is," using abstract, general terms, my words seem simply to fly out without having much impact. But when I begin to enumerate in detail the particular ways in which heat has affected my day, my experience can no longer be easily dismissed. The contributions of spouses and children and parents and fellow workers and fellow students and other people are similarly best examined in detail. But beware! What follow naturally are thoughts of beginning to repay our debts to these supporters. The reflection aspect of Constructive Living ties us into the surrounding world with particular intimacy and the desire for reciprocity.

Traditional psychodynamic Western psychotherapy had an unintended effect on the criminal justice system. While on one level psychologists were trying to understand the psychological causes of criminal behavior, on another level psychotherapists of various sorts were hoping to be able to provide psychological help that would prevent further criminal activity. This unintended effect came about when psychologists thought they had figured out the causes of criminal activity, and when their psychological *explanations* of lawbreaking became a legal and social *excuse* for criminals. When psychotherapists held out the hope to society of "curing" criminals by psychological means, they failed to provide *any* real improvement for the people they originally sought to help.

The results of such errors are apparent for the world to see.

The hope for reducing crime in our country depends on the principle of holding people responsible for their actions. This responsibility is constant and unfailing. Issues of intent and psychological state only line the pockets of forensic psychiatrists and psychologists, lawyers, and judges. The complicated arguments of Western psychotherapy twist the legal system into congested knots.

Once convicted of criminal behavior, the culprits should face the results of their crimes daily. The penal system should include prolonged exposure to videotapes, personal accounts, audiotapes, and written materials concerning the impact of the criminals' actions on the lives of their victims. Criminals should be encouraged to ponder the crises they have caused in others' lives. Rather than being encouraged to search for the causes of the behavior in the errors of family and society, prisoners should be made to look at their own responsibility in causing trouble to the specific people they harmed by their criminal deeds.

Constructive Living, of course, provides just such an opportunity for tough and honest self-reflection. Before I will do any other work with someone convicted of a crime, I require that the person do

Constructive Living reflection on the specific people who were hurt by his or her criminal activities. Exactly what trouble and inconvenience were caused? What were the effects of the crime on the victim's sense of security and personal safety? What amount of time did the victim have to invest in order to proceed with prosecution? What effort was involved? What losses of property were involved? How did those losses affect the quality of life of the victim?

These days it is relatively easy for incarcerated individuals to escape having to endure such reflections by thinking instead about the inconveniences to themselves imposed by the penal system. They may even see themselves as victims through some twist of logic.

Some readers will be surprised to learn that I am not at all interested in producing remorse or guilt or repentance by these means. I am interested in helping criminals to see more clearly the reality of the results of their illegal activities. Having considered the results—not abstractly but in concrete, specific detail—some individuals may choose to give up their lives of crime; others may not. But the decision is now based on having taken an initial look at some of the consequences for others. There is plenty of solid research evidence from Japan that Naikan dramatically reduces recidivism in prison populations. Certainly those who wish to make a careful examination of the grief they have caused others should be given the opportunity to do so. And then restitution would be appropriate. Of course.

7. CAUTIONS

The reflection element in CL is like balancing the checkbook of our lives. However, every time we do it, we discover that we are overdrawn. If you do Constructive Living reflection and your account is overflowing with what you have offered others, and there are few withdrawals (what you have received from others and troubles you caused others), then you aren't yet doing proper reflection. A realistic perspective will invariably result in a life statement with an overdrawn account. Check it out.

It is disturbing to look at an overdrawn account. So the mind has many ways of avoiding the recollections that lead to this reality. Here are some examples of what I call pseudoreflection. They are taken from the reports of Constructive Living students who were *not* doing proper CL reflection in these moments.

What I gave to others:
I gave my mother lots of attention while I was growing up. I went into psychotherapy for my mother's sake; I was able to help my mother by understanding myself.
I did my mother the favor of dropping off my pets whenever I went on vacation; I gave her the chance to be useful.
I did my teachers the favor of listening to what they were teaching.

What I received from others:
My brothers and sisters and I received love from our parents.
We were pretty good kids, so we all got an allowance, though other kids got more money for their allowances.

What troubles I caused others:
I didn't cause any trouble to my father as a child.
Don't forget, I had a high fever at the time.

Reflecting on one's past within a Constructive Living framework sometimes produces amusing results. One fellow arrived at the fascinating conclusion that when he caused a traffic accident, totally destroying his father's car, it might conceivably be considered a trouble he caused his father but it would more properly be considered a favor he did his father. He was, after all, practicing driving so that he could run errands for the family. And his accident gave his father the opportunity to demonstrate his love for the son by buying another car. Following this line of thinking, the father might appropriately thank the son for his car-wrecking

DAVID K. REYNOLDS

favor. How absurd! But such distorted logic isn't uncommon as students twist and turn in order to avoid looking at the great degree to which their lives (and ours) cause inconvenience to others and the meager contributions they (and we) make to others' lives.

Some people cry when they realize how much they have been given and how little they returned to others. How could they have taken so much without recognizing it and thanking their benefactors? How could they have focused so much on the troubles others cause them while ignoring all the difficulties they caused others? But tears won't tell you about the depth of a student's Constructive Living reflection or about the purity or depth of feeling involved. Sometimes tears tell you only that the student is crying.

Once we discover our genuine debt to the world, we may be tempted to use up all our resources immediately in order to begin to repay our debts to others. However, we may be able to repay more and better by using some of our current resources to produce more assets for repayment. As maturity develops, we can develop the ability to delay gratification; similarly we can develop the ability to delay rectification, too, until the proper time. To be sure, putting off making amends can be an excuse, an evasion. In everything there are appropriate times and means.

I want to emphasize that Constructive Living reflection is not an admonition to "look on the bright side" or to "count your blessings." And it is not undertaken for the purpose of creating repentance or the desire for forgiveness or salvation. (Certainly words such as *repentance* and *salvation* are rather unpopular in some circles these days.) It is based simply on the need for seeing more of reality or seeing more realistically. Along with such vision a variety of feelings may well up. That emanation of emotion is understandable, but it is not the goal of our reflection. We are encouraged merely to give up the convenient myths and to behold clearly.

Constructive Living aims at ongoing daily reflection, not a once-in-a-lifetime enlightening experience. Throughout the day we can take time to consider the effects of our actions on others and theirs on us, the balance of giving and receiving. Michael Whitely, a CL instructor in San Francisco, calls this instant Naikan, reflecting in spare moments, while waiting in line, and so forth.

Life may not meet our fantasies of perfection, but it is important to recognize again and again how well reality takes care of us despite our imperfections.

Conversations and Correspondence

1. HOW DO YOU KNOW WHAT NEEDS DOING?

"So the heart of your approach is doing what needs to be done. How do we know what needs to be done? There always seems so much that needs doing. How do we choose?"

"I have no idea."

"You mean that the very center of Constructive Living is a puzzle?"

"Yes, certainly."

"How can you build a lifeway or therapy, or whatever you want to call it, and not understand its central concept?"

"How did you know that question needed to be asked?"

"Well, there are a variety of reasons I could offer."

"Yes. You could talk about an outline of queries you wrote down before this interview or the outline you carry in your mind. You could talk about your past experiences with interviewing of this sort. You could talk about that question bubbling up from your unconscious or from fate or God or reality. The very range and variety of reasons you could marshal makes me suspect them all. Which of them should I accept as satisfying? So the wealth of theories explaining why we do what we do suggests to me that no one has offered one theory superior to all the others; no one knows. However, the reality that you did, in fact, ask the question would be difficult to deny. So even though we don't know the why of it, we can recognize the reality of the action, the doing."

2. THE LEADER IN THE FIELD

"I came to learn about Constructive Living from you because you are the leader in the field."

"Not really. We have the top instructor for Constructive Living right here in the United States today. His name is Professor Genjitsu."

"Professor Genjitsu?"

"Yes."

"How can I get in touch with this Professor Genjitsu?"

"You are indeed fortunate. He is in this building right now. I understand he is willing to teach you about Constructive Living for as long as you wish to study with him, and without charge."

"Did he teach you?"

"Yes, and I still study with him when I'm in the United States and Japan."

"I'd certainly like to meet Mr. Genjitsu."

"Look around. He's right behind you."

"But I don't see anyone."

"Turn around again; he's behind you now."

"But—"

"Oh, yes, and he's in front of you too."

"What?"

"*Genjitsu* is the Japanese word for immediate, present reality— the reality right where you are now. I only teach as one of Professor Genjitsu's representatives. This chair is also his representative, and that window shade and the scrap of plastic wrapping there on the desk. All of them will teach you if you allow them to do so. Professor Reality is a generous and patient teacher. He and his wife, Professor Experience, are a dependable couple, worthy mentors."

DAVID K. REYNOLDS

3. JUST THIS NOW

"Is Constructive Living a philosophy?"

I drop a pen on the floor and pick it up. "This is Constructive Living. Is this a philosophy?"

"But philosophies give organization and meaning to behaviors, and so does Constructive Living."

"When you just spoke to me, you used words that could be analyzed by linguistic analysis. Would that analysis be the same as the words you spoke? Is linguistic theory the same as the words you spoke?"

"No."

"Constructive Living is your speaking, your smiling now, your shaking your head, your nodding. Do you see it?"

4. SATISFACTION'S GUARANTEE

"Don't you hunger for something more in your life?"

"Isn't reality enough?"

"Hmmm. Maybe *your* reality is sufficient."

"It's all we've got, all we are."

"What if I want to change it?"

"Then work to change it."

"It's easier to change it with a pill."

"That changes the way you perceive reality. Reality just keeps flowing along."

"But I feel better about it."

"And feelings fade."

"Then what should I do?"

"You've heard it before, 'Do what needs doing.' "

5. EMPTY CUPS?

"I can understand how reflection on what we have received from others, what we have returned to others, and what troubles we have caused others might work for people who have always had a lot.

But what about those who have little or nothing? What about those who are homeless, without income, without food? What about those who are dying of incurable illness, who were physically and psychologically abused as children?"

"The best answer to your question is to try the reflection aspect of Constructive Living and discover its value. But you want talk, so I'll offer you some words. Constructive Living is not aimed at justifying or preserving the status quo. Again, it is about seeing reality. And there are parts of reality that we humans tend to ignore. We talk, from a distance, about homeless people, for example, having 'nothing.' It isn't so. Humans don't survive with nothing. A warm, safe place to sleep merits appreciation. A meal, whether it is donated by a mission or by a Fortune 500 company, merits gratitude. I am not saying that the leftover stew and the full-course French meal are the same, but I am saying that both are gifts. There is nothing in Constructive Living that prevents us from working to change the sorts of gifts we receive. In fact this constructive lifeway encourages positive action aimed at achieving our goals."

"But what about those who look into their childhood past and find nothing but painful memories?"

"If they look diligently, they are likely to find service and care, too, perhaps even from those who also abused them. That's very important. It shrinks down the giant cardboard devils from the past into more rounded, human-sized people. They lose their imagined power over us in the present."

6. THE PRICE OF SELF-WORTH

"I am in therapy to discover self-worth and empowerment. For years I thought that nothing I ever did or said was worth anything. How can you tell me that the ideal of Constructive Living is to become 'nothing special'?"

"The best way to maximize your potential is to give up your pursuit of self-esteem, check out the way things are, and act accordingly."

"The way things are?"

"Yes, you (like the rest of us) aren't particularly deserving of esteem sometimes. We keep changing. What is trustworthy is reality. Science is based on that principle too. You can count on reality even when you can't count on yourself. In other words, reality keeps right on while we waffle about in our goals and desires and moods."

"But I want to feel good about myself."

"Creating realistic goals and working to achieve them will do more for your self-image than talking about improving it, but I must insist that such a goal is trivial."

"Sometimes I serve and serve my family in the hope that they will recognize my work and appreciate me, but they just take my work for granted. I deserve some recognition for that effort."

"An interesting purpose, isn't it? You serve them in order to get appreciation. It's not service, is it. It's attempted coercion, a kind of manipulation. And you can't control their response, their level of appreciation of your manipulation. Perhaps you should rethink your purpose."

"You mean I should stop serving them?"

"Maybe you should start serving them."

7. IMPOSED LIMITS

"How can you say such things about psychoanalysis?"

"I've worked with psychoanalysts and with their patients; I've read about the subject."

"But have you ever undergone psychoanalysis?"

"No."

"Then you don't really understand it and shouldn't talk about it."

"Let me get this straight. You are arguing that if one hasn't done or been something, it is impossible to understand or talk about it sensibly. Right?"

"Of course."

"Have you ever been a black? a male? over forty? a member of another family? Have you ever been me?"

"Of course not."

"Well, according to your argument, you can't understand or

talk meaningfully about any of these topics. In fact according to your criteria, all you can talk about sensibly is yourself. Seems pretty limited. How can you know I don't understand psychoanalysis when you've never been me?"

8. RESPONSE TO A LETTER FROM A DABBLER

Dear B,
 You are far too satisfied and successful with your bounded life as it is to involve yourself in anything as ordinary/radical as Constructive Living. You have no idea how much you do NEED it. Get in touch again when you are ready to take the plunge.
Sincerely,
David Reynolds

9. RESPONSES TO LETTERS FROM CONSTRUCTIVE LIVING INSTRUCTORS

You are right about the difficulty of practicing the Constructive Lifeway. It is true for all of us. I'm sure your body-mind appreciates the exercise you offer it in the mornings and the services you offer others. This sort of action is the best training and preparation for teaching Constructive Living to your students. It will provide the standard against which you can check whether you are getting the words right when teaching others.

Your life koan—"Hold to *whose* purpose?"—contains enough depth to provide years and years of contemplation. One side path this particular koan has led you to is the question from your letter "But am I not the person who interprets reality?" When you want to walk along this side path, you must ask yourself, "Who is this person who interprets reality?" Look for the person just as you look for the purpose. In other words, at various times during the day notice your purpose in some ongoing activity and examine where that purpose came from. That examination can be philosophical and rational, as in the answers you gave to me in your letter, but

DAVID K. REYNOLDS

it must also be experiential, phenomenological—that is, look for the source of your purpose of the moment; search for the purpose's earliest glimmering in your mind. Where, how, when does it arise? To whom does it belong? I can assure you it isn't simply yours, either in the simpler sense you already understand or in another sense. Just look now and again.

PART II

APPLICATIONS

Maxims

Maxims are ways of using words to remind ourselves of Constructive Living principles. Language is a useful tool, albeit in some ways a dangerous one. We must often remind ourselves that words about reality aren't the reality itself.

Constructive Living is like a language. Once a language is learned, it can never be totally forgotten. You can never return to a condition in which the sounds are a meaningless jumble as they were before you began your study of the language. You can never see your everyday life as you did before beginning your study of Constructive Living.

Whether you are completely fluent in Constructive Living or not, you retain your ability to use this view of life to make sense of your world. More than that, once you have some fundamental grasp of the principles (the grammar and vocabulary, if you like), you *cannot* completely set them aside.

Constructive Living is not merely another language; Constructive Living is your *native* language.

Here are more words about this Constructive Living language:

There is reality's work only *you* can do.

No need for perfection—reality loves you anyway.

Digging out the old; new construction zone.

Have you been through enough to appreciate reality when you see it?

Reality's blossom. On-purpose blooming. Which bud?

Knows how to fly; learning to walk.

Happy birthday, Mom. Without yours I wouldn't have one. Love, Your Child.

If it's raining and you have an umbrella, use it, even if the umbrella is tattered and imperfect.

If it's raining and you have an umbrella, use it, but it's hard to type with an umbrella in your hand.

The tiny wilted white ginger blossoms in the plastic margarine container of water nevertheless give a pleasing fragrance to the room.

Constructive Living—when you care to *do* the very best.

If alcohol is your koan, solve it.

I've had lots of troubles in my life, and most of them never happened. —David Miles

Run to the edge of the cliff and stop on a dime, then thank those who helped you get to the dime. —David Miles

When the seas are stormy, thank the boatmaker and keep on rowing. —Henry Kahn

Have you thanked your guilt today? —Sheila Sabrey-Saperstein

Over there is not here. —Andrew Kumasaka

Reality never tires, only you do. —Daniel Hoppe

A Ph. Do is more useful than a Ph.D. —Rose Anderson

Reality school—where you're on a scholarship even though you are flunking, but you never get to repeat a course. —Rose Anderson

Ears hear more than thoughts do. —Fred Ketchum

Have now, will travel. —Deanna Kirk

Trust the ground beneath your feat. —Deanna Kirk

Come to your senses. —Deanna Kirk

Do think then thank. —Deanna Kirk

The steps to climb Mount Everest and the steps to climb a small hill are the same size. —Robert Orenstein

Today is for-giving. —Patricia Ryan-Madson

In every moment opportunities for action. In every action opportunities for thanks. —Robert Orenstein

Purposeful access. (Here is a simple principle that is useful for making what needs doing more likely to occur. Make easily available those things that are useful in accomplishing your purpose and put those things that are harmful out of reach. For example, if you want to lift weights as part of your daily exercise routine, keep the weights out and handy, don't force yourself to dig them out of the back of the garage or closet each time you want to use them. Conversely those things you don't want to use should be hard to get to—tobacco, alcohol, fattening foods, and credit cards might be examples of such things.)

Koans

Koans are about making mental leaps. The koan practice helps train the mind to find certain kinds of essences in everyday life. If these essences are pointed out to the student, they may be appreciated, but to explain them outright gives the student no chance to make the mental leap alone. To explain a koan to a student would be rather like reading a book of chess problems while consulting the answer pages instead of working out the answers without help. The doing itself produces some skill and persistence.

Koans are puzzles that keep the mind occupied, teaching basic principles in novel ways. It is best to ponder Constructive Living koans over a span of time, one at a time. When one puzzle is mastered or when you are blocked after a couple of weeks working on a Constructive Living koan, move along to the next one. A well-constructed (well-discovered) koan has layers of meaning. Below I have written some koans in prose and some in poetic form. Answers can be confirmed by certified Constructive Living instructors. Answers are right or wrong and do not depend on the subjective evaluation of the student. An answer that begins "For me the meaning of this koan is . . ." is wrong.

THE UNKNOWN

A young man keeps sending postcards to his faraway lover as he travels. He is unaware that his lover has written to his home informing him that she is leaving him for another. He won't get her letter until he returns months later from his extended trip. Were his postcards written for nothing?

THE LEMON MERINGUE PIE

A man enters a room, walks over to a chair with a lemon meringue pie on it, and sits down on the pie. After a time a second man enters the room saying, "I don't like what I am about to do, but I can't seem to help myself from doing it. Furthermore I do understand some of the underlying reasons for this act." Then he walks over to the chair and sits on a lemon meringue pie too. A third fellow, after sitting on a lemon meringue pie, rises to say, "What an uncomfortable yet vital lesson I have learned from this experience." Then he proceeds to sit on yet another lemon meringue pie. What is the difference among these men? What is the similarity?

EAT, SLEEP

What Constructive Living sense can we make of Zen psychology's advice to "Eat when hungry; sleep when tired"? The Zen maxim cannot have the transparent meaning it appears to have. Imagine that a visitor comes for dinner and there isn't enough food for visitor and family. Because one is hungry, should one ignore the visitor's needs or convenience and eat anyway?

One sort of Constructive Living sense we can make of the advice to "Eat when hungry; sleep when tired" is that there is no need to look for deep, hidden, complex motivations underlying simple acts. Such concerns with complex searches simply distract us from doing what needs doing. Can you find other Constructive Living interpretations in this maxim?

ALARM

My portable computer alarm flashes "now" . . . "now" . . . "now."
And beneath the current time it flashes "goal" . . . "goal" . . . "goal."
The time for which the alarm is set.
Reminders of what is, not what will be.

ASSORTED BRIEF KOANS

1. Nothing to Spare

What is wrong and right about throwing leftovers from the refrigerator and not finishing all the food on the plate as methods of losing weight? What is better? What broader meaning can you find in this koan?

2. Getting Together

How am I getting along with my dishes? What is the purpose of developing intimacy with things as well as people?

3. Puzzle Box

Discover the meaning underlying these words written by Ron Green:

The whole world is living us. This chair is doing its chairness, aside from my opinions and notions about it. It is alive in its chairness. If one puts aside one's self and sees what is—there is just reality.

The self we think we are is a nonself made up of all the selves in the universe.

DAVID K. REYNOLDS

Exercises

Constructive Living has been criticized by some Japanese Morita therapists for our assignment of exercises. These Japanese Moritists hold that Morita's approach aims at finding meaning in ordinary everyday life, not in artificially created exercises. However, I see these assignments as intermediary steps to mindful daily living, just as vacuuming as distraction from immediate suffering is an intermediary step toward the ultimate end of vacuuming to get the room clean. Exercises provide novelty and learning opportunities at an accelerated pace. While one is in Constructive Living training, exercises are part of "ordinary everyday living." Reality might send you similar lessons over time anyway, naturally. In either case, be alert to learn from them.

No one knows which means are the most expedient or effective for teaching Constructive Living to a particular student. Frankly we can't predict well at all which teaching devices will produce results for our students. Which tale, which assignment, which maxim, which concept will nudge or boot someone into a moment of genuine understanding of this practice? So we set out the information cafeteria-style, hoping you will select what you need from the servings before you. Here are some experiential exercises from the Constructive Living cafeteria:

GIVE YOURSELF AWAY

Patricia Ryan Madson, a faculty member of Stanford University, suggests to her Constructive Living students that they give away something every day. A number of other Constructive Living instructors work on clearing away the material overload that plagues their lives by offering items that still have a useful life to others.

A DATING GAME

Patricia Ryan Madson also recommends to her students who seek to socialize more that they invite others to go with them to do ordinary chores, such as shopping, laundry, washing the car, and so forth. Such expeditions must be done anyway and don't carry the formality of a date. People deserve to be invited whether they accept the invitation or not.

GROUP REWARDS

Gregg Krech, a Constructive Living instructor and management consultant, works not only on rewarding individuals for good performance but on rewarding an entire work group for achieving some stated goal through cooperative effort.

CREDIT WHERE IT IS DUE

Gregg Krech also suggests selecting your finest accomplishment in life for reflection and discovering the specific contributions of others that allowed you to accomplish that feat. Similarly he recommends that you consider the specific support of others when you were at your lowest point in life.

DAVID K. REYNOLDS

ADMIRATION WHERE IT IS DUE

Another of Gregg Krech's exercises is to write the name of the person you admire most. Then write what you admire most about that person. You will find that under whatever you find admirable about that person is what he or she does, his or her behavior. What makes people admirable is what they do. To become admirable people, we must do admirable doings. The exercise can be extended by interviewing other people and discovering their most admired person and the reasons for that esteem.

SETTING GOALS

Dr. Ishu Ishiyama, at the University of British Columbia, offers this assignment to his students: Come up with a life goal, then write down what you can do in the next five years to help achieve that goal. Then write down what you can do this year, this month, this week, today.

ENCOMPASS CRITICISM

Make a special effort to be accepting of criticism. Find the truth in criticism, the beautiful source beneath it. Don't allow yourself to be so distracted by the hurt or the form the cricitism takes that you miss the positive information it contains. The Taoist approach to what appears at first to be a lie is to discover the truth underlying the words. "I never make mistakes" may mean "I dread making mistakes" or "I find it hard to look at my imperfection." Take the same approach to criticism. Similarly Morita offered this advice about advice: Thank the person who offers it, but you have no obligation to follow it. Do the same with criticism.

CHARTING DAILY ACTIVITIES

We may distance ourselves from reality with words. We may say to ourselves and to others that we have no time for some important projects. We may complain that we seem to accomplish little or nothing in our everyday lives. We may hold that life is boring, that we are lazy, that there is too much to do or not enough to do.

This exercise allows you to check on the reality of your everyday activities. It offers an objective record of what you are doing at fifteen-minute intervals during the day. *Shufu no Tomo,* a Japanese women's magazine with an associated nationwide organization, encourages its membership to chart a daily activities inventory. The members graph how they spend their time (and how much money is spent on what activities). It is an exercise well worth a try. You may find that there are substantial periods of time in between other activities, time that can be used more effectively.

The procedure is simple to explain. Make a twenty-four-hour chart with fifteen-minute intervals marked and space for writing a brief word or two about what you did during each interval. Words such as *eating, running, sleeping, watching TV, cooking, reading, lounging, waxing car,* and the like are sufficient. Keep an ongoing record during the day; don't try to recall the whole day's activities before bedtime. However, you may find it impractical to interrupt some activity to chart it. When the activity ends, catch up on the charting. Continue the daily charting for a week.

NEW YEAR'S DAY ACTIVITY

On New Year's Day try writing your epitaph, obituary, and eulogy as you might wish them to be if you were to die during the year. They should contain an account of your life accomplishments to date and your plans for the coming year. It is a good way to remind yourself of the limited time within which you must do what needs doing. The same exercise might be repeated on your birthday and the results compared each year. The exercise is not about death itself but about what you will accomplish before death.

DAVID K. REYNOLDS

GIVE A PARTY

1. Make the theme a cleanup of the beach or a nearby park. Then provide refreshments and entertainment at the cleaned-up site.
2. Invite your friends to a quilting bee or some modern equivalent during which you make something to give away to the homeless, a nursing home, a mental institution, an orphanage. Check with people who have everyday contact with these institutions for an appropriate party purpose.
3. Throw a gardening party for a convalescing or new neighbor. Invite friends to weed the garden and shrubs and to mow the lawn. Then have a barbecue.

GOING PLACES

Pick an occasion such as your birthday or anniversary or holiday for this exercise. Write down where you expect to be and what you expect to be doing six months later and one year later. Write down some of the behavioral steps you must take to achieve those goals. Then put away these notes in a safe place with instructions to open them the same time next year. Check on how well you did. What goals were achieved? What steps went unaccomplished? Then write your expectations for the following year and repeat the process.

We do this exercise as a family project at my sister's home at Christmas. We open last year's folded sheets and read aloud our expectations. There is sometimes laughter as we compare what we expected with current reality.

REMINDERS

On a dozen notes write the question "What is my purpose now?" Post them in various places where you are apt to notice them during the day (for example, on the phone, the calendar, a doorknob, a file cabinet, the refrigerator, the television). As you come across the notes, consider whether you are doing what is necessary to accomplish your pupose. (Suggested by Daniel Hoppe.)

GARBAGE GRATITUDE

Write a letter to the company that collects your trash praising its trash collectors for some specific service they have provided you, such as taking the trash cans out of the enclosure when you forgot to set them by the curb. (Suggested by Daniel Hoppe.)

SCRAMBLED ACTS

Scramble the order in which you wash yourself in the shower, perform your morning toilet, eat breakfast, prepare for bed. The new order will require attention. (Suggested by Daniel Hoppe.)

IMPERFECTION

Within ten minutes write down thirty of your accomplishments, great or small, from anything as simple as eating a sandwich to other things as long-term as completing a college degree. Put a check by those things you did perfectly. Notice how many of your accomplishments have been achieved even though you did them imperfectly, even though you may consider yourself a perfectionist. (Suggested by Rose Anderson.)

RECIPROCITY

Do a secret service (a service, however small, to someone without him knowing you did it for him) for the third (or fourth or fifth) person who does something for you after you put down this book. (Adapted from a suggestion by Gregg Krech.)

DAVID K. REYNOLDS

TAKE A HIKE

It will take quite a few steps to work off the calories in a bite of pastry. Why not start walking even before you take a bite? Fred Paterno suggests moving your feet as though already on your walk INSTEAD OF taking that bite. By the time he gets to about sixty paces, Fred finds his enthusiasm for eating pastries has diminished.

KEEPING TRACK

A convenient way for keeping track of whether you got in your minimum ten thank-yous every day is suggested by Gregg Krech: Put ten pebbles or coins in your left pocket, and with each thank-you transfer one to your right pocket.

GETTING IT TOGETHER

Check out your understanding of Constructive Living by preparing a fifteen-minute speech about CL to be presented to a specified audience of your choice. (Adapted from a suggestion by Barbara Sarah.)

COMPARATIVE SERVICE

Offer two acts of service—one when feeling grateful to someone and the other when feeling no gratitude toward that person. How are the acts different? (Suggested by Barbara Sarah.)

CLEAR SEPARATION

Repeat the following sentence several times: "David Reynolds (the name of a Constructive Living instructor or any adviser may be substituted here) is sometimes stupid, sometimes wrong." If you notice resistance to saying these words, you misunderstand Constructive Living. If you say them with some glee, do more CL reflection. If you repeated the sentences in a matter-of-fact way with a sense of "of course," then it is likely that you have properly separated the Constructive Living lifeway (or advice) from the adviser.

Quiz

Because Constructive Living is an educational process, it is appropriate to offer students quizzes now and then. The questions below present the opportunity to think more deeply about Constructive Living concerns. Some hints at ways to begin to think about answers follow, but it is best to ponder the questions well before turning to the hints.

1. How do I know whether this is an impulse or an awareness of what needs doing?
2. How do I know whether confrontation and an assertive posture are necessary here in this situation or not?
3. How do I know whether I am in love or not?
4. What parts of reality must I accept without trying to affect them and what parts should I act to change?
5. Where do decisions come from?
6. What needs doing when someone I care about is destroying himself/herself?
7. Why am I facing this reality now? What is the purpose of it all?

8. When is anger appropriate?
9. How can I get myself to accept whatever feelings emerge?
10. How do I know when to move from one task to another?
11. How can I be sure I reuse old things to give them new life and not because I am cheap?
12. When I do Constructive Living reflection on the past, how can I be sure my mind isn't inventing memories or recalling what I've been told by others to fit my expectations?

Extra-credit questions: How important are these questions in your everyday life? How do your answers affect the way you live today? Is consideration of these issues what needs doing now?

HINTS FOR DIRECTING THOUGHTS ON THE ABOVE QUESTIONS:

1. Look at my past experience, consider probable consequences, do and see.
2. What is my purpose? What are the likely results?
3. Is the well-being of my partner uppermost? What am I willing to give up for that person? Whose convenience am I considering?
4. Is it changeable? Is it changeable by my efforts (and those of others)? What else needs doing?
5. At least two sorts of answers are appropriate here. One answer comes from the circumstances, the situation, the environment. The other answer comes from observation or introspection of the mind generating decisions.
6. What is controllable? What is not?
7. Both the reflection and the action aspects of CL lead you to answers to this question.
8. When is hunger appropriate? When is love appropriate? When is sorrow appropriate? When are tides and snowflakes and breezes appropriate?
9. How can I get myself to accept hunger when I am hungry?

DAVID K. REYNOLDS

How can I get myself to accept drowsiness when I've been awake twenty-four hours?

10. Is a task completed? Is there something else that is more important to do? Am I wasting time on this task?

11. How else do I use money? Do I give new life to things that wouldn't cost me much (or anything) new?

12. Ask others from my past. Examine written documents and photographs. Nevertheless I can't be sure of the details from the distant past. Do Constructive Living reflection on what was received from others, returned to others, and on the troubles caused others today.

PART III
TALES OF CONSTRUCTIVE LIVING

In Constructive Living tales have a number of purposes. They teach, of course, the principles of this lifeway. Inoculation tales are designed to prepare the student for future tragedies, shocks, dilemmas. Insight tales are designed to help students see themselves more clearly. Jolting tales aim at challenging some unrealistic but commonly held view. Like maxims, tales code Constructive Living messages in readily remembered form.

I am pleased to be able to include in this section, too, contributions from my Constructive Living colleagues.

Fluff

This is a story about cloud people. Cloud people float in the sky on word clouds. They drift mindlessly on soft pink syllables.

Large cumulus clouds are composed of phrases like "mystery unfolding in you," "you are God in action," "give yourself permission to be in that special magical inner place," "there is beauty and joy in everything," "celebrate yourself," "you are the Star," "you deserve a wonderful life," "it is your right as God," "you can create anything," "be a gift to the world," "allow the child in you to emerge and demonstrate your beauty and wonderment." Scattered cirrus clouds are made up of words like *effortless, centered, trusting, wondrous, magical, wisdom, healthy, successful, perfect, love, abundance, transform, energy, whole, complete, perfection, peace, joy.* The clouds offer an attractive formation sailing through the sky. But they have no substance up there in the ether.

Hiking is more difficult than sailing on clouds. It isn't nearly as much fun to weave one's way on foot through jungles and prairies as it is to drift in the sun. Climbing a mountain is hard work.

But clouds don't sail their riders over mountains, they rain.

Cloud people know that they aren't anchored to reality. They must know it. Reality keeps reminding them. Still they suspend their disbelief. They call to one another from their vaporous mounts that thinking so makes it so. They encourage others to float up for a ride in the sky. They demonstrate to us the capacity of humans to desperately believe.

Yet thunder and lightning are as real as love. And a shelter built with one's hands offers more protection in a storm than a shelter imaged and affirmed from a celestial perch.

Hazards of Brilliance

Once upon a changing time there lived a street-wise fellow who knew the ropes of therapy too. Let's call him Jaime. Jaime was a quick-witted fellow who knew himself through and through. He knew the games he played with himself and others. He knew intimately his strengths and weaknesses. He knew his unlimited potential.

Jaime wanted to go hiking in the mountains, but he never did. He knew the mental obstacles he threw up to impede his accomplishing his goal. He recognized the mental chatter about the hassle of getting equipment together, the difficulty of assuring comfort and safety on a mountain trail, the problem of being in less than ideal physical condition, and so on. He knew he could get out on the trail in spite of his mental vacillation.

Sometimes Jaime would sit back in a favorite recliner in his den and smile at himself and his foolishness. What an intricate and devious mind he had! But he was aware of all its tricks. He could identify each gambit, each ploy. How well he knew himself, sitting there in the recliner.

One day Jaime opened a book about Constructive Living and read the following passage:

Some very clever people have trouble grasping the essence of Constructive Living. They have been so successful at figuring things out that they overlook the simple action-orientation of this lifeway. They have become so good at seeing through their own life games that they think the seeing alone is sufficient. They are insightful and stuck in their sagacity. Too much dependence on the intellect and an obsession with insight can actually interfere with the experiential understanding of this lifeway.

Jaime closed the book, smiled, and understood exactly what the passage meant. Then he closed his eyes and drifted off to sleep.

Another Chance

At last the new psychotherapeutic technique was perfected. The time machine Model 1.00 stood in stainless-steel splendor next to the traditional padded couch. Anne sat on the couch musing about the possibilities. Her therapist coughed gently a couple of times.

"Anne . . . Anne."

"Oh, yes. Sorry, Dr. Kirschner. I got lost in the possibilities of doing it all over—and doing it right this time." Anne looked cheerful for the first time in a long time.

"Remember, Anne. If you are to go through this therapeutic time regression, so must your parents. You cannot do it alone. They must agree to go back twenty years in the past with you. As soon as they have agreed and signed the waiver, we can begin training your family to engage in more functional childrearing. We can reshape the roots of your character."

"Oh, Doctor. Isn't it wonderful! I'm sure they will agree. They can undo all the harm they did to me with their poor parenting. They will have the chance to be twenty years younger again. How could they refuse?"

To Anne's surprise, however, her parents did refuse. They told her that nothing could make them want to relive the heartaches of those turbulent years of her childhood and adolescence, not even their love for her.

At first Anne was terribly disappointed and hurt. Then she began to consider the implications of the reason for her parents' refusal. Dr. Kirschner was not so surprised. Once more he cleaned the light film of dust that had accumulated on Model 1.00.

Grindstone Cowboy

Once upon a Western time there was a ranch owner, Carl, who overworked. From sunup to sundown he was riding herd or doing the books or rounding up new employees for his ten-thousand-acre business. He was too busy to give his wife a birthday gift, too busy to attend his son's graduation ceremony, too busy to have medical checkups, too busy to notice that his Mercedes's speedometer seldom dropped below eighty miles per hour.

One of the ranch hands was reading a book about Constructive Living in the bunkhouse. He thought Carl was a good example of a Constructive Living person. Certainly Carl kept busy, didn't seem to be squandering his time. Wasn't that what Constructive Living was all about—keeping active?

Chasing a Phantasm

For years the alchemists of the mind sought this elusive formula that would turn the human mind to gold. Their incantations and formulations took many forms. But residues and impurities abounded in their test tubes. Lead remained lead; sulfur, sulfur.

So intent were the alchemists on producing pure gold that they lost sight of the value of lead and sulfur and tin and nickel and other base elements. They lost sight of the common earth from which these elements spring.

For all their sincere efforts and long, detailed research, little gold was actually produced. And that which did appear instantly oxidized into ordinary iron.

In time the alchemists came to appreciate the uses of all the elements and gave up their search for pure gold. It took some while to rewrite their manuals. But the earth has time, the mind has time.

The Dancing Lesson

by Patricia Ryan-Madson

On the dance floor Mrs. Tara, the curly-red-haired instructor, announced brightly, "Today, the waltz!" She smiled, pressing the button on the elaborate tape deck of the fine stereo system in the ballroom. The strains of "The Emperor's Waltz," by Strauss, filled the room. Martha sighed with pleasure. More than anything she wanted to learn to dance with a partner, *more than anything*.

"You must learn two skills as you dance together," explained Mrs. Tara. "The first is attention to your footsteps and to those of your partner. You must always continue to notice where you are stepping, carefully doing your best to avoid treading on your partner as you go. Particularly while you are learning, this attention takes a great deal of effort.

"The second skill is the development of an attitude of cheerful tolerance when your partner steps on your toes. You must be understanding and compassionate toward your partner's mistakes. If he knows that you can accept his mistakes without jeopardizing the dance, he can dance with greater freedom. Of course you realize that no matter how sincerely you practice, you *will* step on one another. Stepping on each other unintentionally is in the nature of dancing. You cannot learn to dance without doing so. It is useful to adopt the viewpoint that your partner is doing the best he can.

"Again, if you want to dance you must accept the inevitability of being stepped on occasionally—it is in the nature of the experience of moving closely together. So, shall we begin?"

Martha took a deep breath, smiled, and lifted her arms to Harold, her class partner. Off they glided, or rather bumped, onto the floor. One, two, three; one, two, three; *one,* two three—

"Oops, oh, excuse me," sputtered Harold as he crunched the tip of Martha's patent leather pump.

"That's all right," said Martha soothingly, really meaning it. One, two, three; one, two, three . . . and on they moved, fumbled, smiled, stumbled, laughed, apologized. And sometimes they even really, really danced.

COMMENTARY

Whenever human beings become partners, it is natural that some conflict occurs. It is unrealistic to imagine that partners should move smoothly and perfectly without incident. Mrs. Tara's advice was sound. Knowing that this jostling is likely to happen prepares partners to develop a healthy, charitable attitude toward having their toes stepped on. If your purpose is to build a strong and loving partnership, it would be wise to attend to your own and your partner's footsteps as they fall.

Fairy Tale

by Sheila Sabrey-Saperstein

Once upon a time there was a land called Feelgood. Its rulers were King Happy and Queen Content. They had a court jester named Gut, whose job was to help them make decisions and warn them of danger. The main threat that Gut felt was from those nearby rulers, King Purpose and Queen Action of Clearlook.

King Purpose and Queen Action often assured those in Feelgood that they would never invade their land, for all they were interested in was doing what needed doing in their own kingdom. They wanted to get along well with their neighbors.

One day when Gut was hanging around the castle feeling bored with no decisions on the agenda for that day, he began thinking about Queen Action and King Purpose. The more he thought about them, the more he got an intuitive reaction that they were up to no good, that their activities were a danger to Feelgood.

Gut ran to King Happy and Queen Content and signaled an alarm. Watch out! The kingdom of Clearlook is invading our territory! The king and queen of Feelgood felt their very existence was on the line. If King Purpose and Queen Action took over their country, they would lose their identities, disappear.

Meanwhile the fearful activity in Feelgood and the simple daily tasks in Clearlook were being observed by a lovely golden bird named Naikan. The bird flew between the two countries, nesting in both. The Naikan bird genuinely cared for the people in both countries. The disturbance in Feelgood forebode trouble in both lands.

Fortunately the Naikan bird was able to bring the rulers from both countries together and assist them in tearing down the walls between their realms. Thus, thanks to all concerned, a war was averted.

Trapped

Charley was fifty-five and tired. He had been selling all day. He took a moment to loosen his tie and relax in the recliner at Woods'

Department Store. Charley fell asleep. Somehow the store closed with no one noticing Charley's slumbering form in the furniture section.

When he awoke, the bright morning sunlight forced him to keep his eyes nearly shut while he figured out what and where and how. No one else was in the store. Charley walked to the front window and saw no cars or people moving in the street. He tried the handle on the door, but it wouldn't budge. The phone worked, but no one answered his calls, even when he dialed random numbers. He pulled out the phone directory and tried the local hospital and police station. No answer.

Something had taken people away while Charley slept. Suddenly he was less anxious to leave this haven. Perhaps there was poison gas or radiation or something outside. Charley decided to settle down for a while. After all, there was a huge food section, running water, a selection of comfortable beds and sofas, books and records and videos and an electrical system that seemed to be working properly. Only people were missing.

Not a bad life, thought Charley. I wonder how long it will last. . . .

Six months later Charley dictated the following message into a tape recorder:

Everything is taken care of for me. The electricity still operates, the water still runs. There's plenty of food and clothing and all the material goods I worked so hard to possess. The life of leisure I dreamed about is mine.

But a strange guilt possesses me and an unease. Why was I singled out for this life? Who can I thank for it? Who can I repay for it? And what happened to all the others? Did they have to give up their lives so I could have this material paradise?

I always considered myself something of a loner. Before this I lived alone, kept my ties simple. Now I feel lonely for the first time. I want someone to be around, someone who will talk with me, someone I can do things for. What good is all this stuff? It just keeps me going until I die.

Who am I kidding? This is no Eden. I hate this existence! I long for the hard-work days of my circuit, for the small victories of new orders, for the collection plate at church, for the panhandlers and Gary at the corner newsstand.

Everything I do here I do for me. I'm tired of it. It's been weeks since I shaved, days since I bathed. Why bother? It's just for me. Even writing in this journal is just for me.

But I hope, someday, someone will read these words. Long after I'm gone, perhaps. Read them well! All the things are here. I'm not sick; I'm not bored. And I wonder how much longer I can go on. . . .

Caves

He lived on the surface as a child, but gradually he entered the caves. Year by year he explored farther and farther within the labyrinth. It was pitch-black within the caves. He touched the walls. Sometimes he crawled, one hand stretched before his face. Occasionally he felt and smelled other people moving within the caves. For a while he held hands with a girl, but they became separated.

Glowworms within the caves gave off eerie flashes of light at sporadic intervals. Their combined effect was like that of a flashbulb going off. It was blinding after the long days of blackness. Despite the startling and even painful nature of the flashes, people in the caves longed for them, cherished them. They remembered daylight. Even those who had been born in the caves without ever going out remembered daylight.

The deeper he descended into the maze of tunnels, the quieter it became. And the temperature became constant, neither warming nor cooling with day or night or season on the planet's surface. In the depths he stumbled on skeletons, so he knew that to stay there meant death. Something within him pushed him back toward the surface whenever he wandered into the depths. He wasn't ready to die.

For years he probed the dark and hidden courses of the caves. He drew maps of their meandering spirals and posted charts near the entrance. Some people collected his maps as they would butterflies. Some used the charts to assist in their own exploration of the caves. Some drew better maps based on their investigations of tunnels he never knew.

He asked himself if he could sometime retire from wandering through the caves. Would the memories of exploration ever become sufficient? Or would he retire by descending into the depths to die in the peaceful stability there?

For the moment, however, it was enough to roam the passageways and record his rambling course. The caves deserved to be charted.

The Porcelain Box

by Patricia Stewart

A young woman, Margaret, was given a porcelain box when she graduated from college and moved away to get her first job. The box was a family heirloom; it contained the family's purpose—to work and earn money.

She set the box on a small dresser in her new home. Margaret could see her reflection in it; she could see who she was. Because it was very important for her to check on who she was, Margaret polished the box frequently and vigorously. One day the box fell off the dresser and broke. Margaret picked up the pieces carefully and put them away. She couldn't find any scattered contents of the box, however.

Despair and emptiness came. She couldn't polish the box and she couldn't verify who she was. Margaret decided to replace the porcelain box.

The clay from which the box was created was extremely scarce. Margaret took a class in molding and firing porcelain boxes. She studied with an instructor who knew the methods of painting and glazing.

She was still depressed. She had the skills to mold, paint, glaze, and fire the box, but she couldn't find the special clay to make it, even though she wrote a letter each day seeking that necessary material. And she kept practicing her skills.

One day a rather shabby old man made a surprising delivery.

He handed her a package of the special clay. Margaret thanked him. Then she proceeded to make a new box from the clay.

When it was polished, she looked at its surface to see who she was. She discovered that she wasn't quite the same as before.

Margaret reflected that without the old man's gift or without her skills the new box wouldn't have come into being. She looked around her and saw much that could be put within the functional or purposeful space within the box.

So Darn Cute

Lani was tired of being so darn cute. You might think that being cute is a great advantage for a young lady, but there are disadvantages too. You have to keep wondering about people's purposes and about whether you maintain your cuteness quotient with them. Appearance is very important, and perkiness and cleverness and sophistication and talent and so on. Imagine living every day in a sort of beauty pageant. As you get older, the comparisons get tougher and it takes more effort to stay competitive. Not a lot of fun, after all.

Lani was a bright girl, however, and she wanted to opt out of the race for Miss Cuteness of Every Year. How could she go about it? She decided to give her cuteness to the world as a gift. It wasn't hers anyway. She presented her perky smile and sparkling eyes as offerings to brighten up the moments when people talked with her or just walked by. In other words, she dropped from the pageant to take another job, but she kept her looks and her pertness skills as assets for giving to her new clients. By the way, giving away one's beauty is not the same as giving away one's body.

Beauty queens are usually in the race for themselves. Truly beautiful people aren't.

The Slippery Throat

Once upon a time there was a little girl, Phyllis, with a slippery throat. Words slipped out of her throat so rapidly that sometimes she was surprised at what she said. Someone had told her that people didn't like little girls who are wishy-washy, so no matter how strange the words that slipped from her throat, she never took them back.

She stood by her words no matter what. Everyone around her thought she was very bright because her words came out so quickly; no one ever suspected her of lying because she didn't have time to make up any falsehood—her replies came too quickly for that. And Phyllis hated to make people wait for her answers to their questions. Furthermore, in some families if you don't get your words in quickly, somebody else will jump into the conversation with theirs. A slippery throat has some advantages.

Unfortunately sometimes the words that flew from the little girl's lips weren't the words she would have liked to say. Sometimes they were even wrong. But words won't slide back down the throat easily; they can't be swallowed at all. What to do?

Sometimes Phyllis pretended she was a wall and couldn't hear or speak at all. But that was no fun, and people knew better. Sometimes Phyllis put lots of food in her mouth so that she wouldn't have to speak—good girls don't speak with their mouths full, you know.

As Phyllis grew up, she learned to give word-package presents to others. She learned to wrap up her word gifts in just the right wrappings before offering them. It took a little more time to make them presentable, but when they slipped from her throat, they fit the occasion beautifully. What a gift!

Bite-Sized

Dale was a reasonable sort of a guy who liked to have a handle on things. He saw himself as open-minded and sensible with a good balance of imagination and practicality. And he was right. Especially as life moved along pretty smoothly.

Dale worried sometimes, though, what might happen to his nicely disciplined flexibility if tragedy struck. Would he be able to handle the sudden pressures? Would he fall back to old habits of aiming to run away from reality's disasters?

Then tragedy struck. And Dale felt an unexpected sense of relief amid the suffering—it was only tragedy, after all. You see, Dale discovered that real crises are only as big as they are. Imagined crises are infinitely large.

Weakest Link

by Daniel Hoppe

In a kingdom long ago Hans, the official rope maker, made all the ropes for everyone. He wove hemp into good, strong rope according to official standards.

One wintry Friday night Hans was impatient to get home and spend some time with Torborg, his old friend from a neighboring land. On such a snowy night the mulled wine that Torborg made would taste especially good.

Hans was working on his last rope of the day—a colorful, decorative rope that was to be used in an exhibit in the Royal Museum. Although he wanted to get home early, it looked like the rope would keep him at his bench later than usual. Just then Hans recalled an old rope-making shortcut he had heard about as an apprentice. The result wouldn't meet standards and it might be seriously weak, but what the hell, it was only for decoration anyway.

Using the shortcut, Hans finished the rope in half the normal time. Bundling himself up against the cold, Hans coiled and packed the rope for delivery and tossed it into his wagon. Then he hopped aboard and headed off in the snow.

The road to the Royal Museum was on his way home. It ran alongside the lip of a steep ravine. As Hans's wagon moved across a particularly narrow stretch of road, it slid sideways on a patch of ice, hit a tree, and pitched Hans over the edge of the ravine. Fortunately Hans was able to grab a jutting tree root and keep himself from falling to his death on the rocks below.

He dangled there for what seemed an eternity until he heard a reassuring voice calling from above.

"Don't worry," the voice shouted. "We'll save you. There was a rope in your wagon. Just grab hold of the end and we'll have you up here in no time."

Sensitivity and Sense

Lila was told she was incapable of loving. By the very man she loved with all her heart. She believed him.

DAVID K. REYNOLDS

Craig no longer loved Lila; he loved someone else. So it was convenient for Craig to tell Lila she didn't really love him. When Lila objected, Craig got mad. What a hassle this was turning out to be!

"You can't love anyone but yourself!" he snapped at her.

And she believed him.

There was no doubt in Lila's mind that she did love herself. She thought about herself a lot; she protected herself; she wanted the best for herself. Craig must be right. She loved only herself.

Lila needed an ear operation—her hearing was poor. Craig needed a speech therapist—his speech was dysfunctional.

Distraction

by Deanna Kirk

Little Dede was afraid to go to the doctor's office. She cried on the way. The doctor noticed her fear. He asked her what was her favorite thing in the whole world.

"It's my doll," said Dede.

"That's fine," the doctor went on, "How long have you known her?"

"A long time."

"What is she wearing today?"

"A red dress."

"I see. Where does she live?"

"In her house in my bedroom," replied Dede. "When will I get a shot?"

"It's already done," said the doctor. "You can go home and tell your doll about it."

Train Tale

When you get on a train, it is important to have your destination in mind. If you board the train in Chicago and wish to go to Los Angeles, you must not board a train headed for New York. No matter how long you ride the train headed for New York, you won't arrive in Los Angeles. No matter how speedy and modern the train, no matter how clever the passengers, no matter how many of your friends are passengers on the train, if it is headed for New York, you can't take it to Los Angeles. Know where you want to go. Then take steps to get there.

This train is crowded. A young man stands in the aisle of this coach. He has been standing for over an hour. He boarded the train late, after the seats were already filled.

Three people were occupying the seats next to where he stands, but long ago they went off to the lounge car for a snack. He stands by empty seats.

Now, just as he is about to sit down, they return.

Those who have get more. Those who have not encounter difficulty getting anything at all. It appears to lie in the timing.

How long will he stand? When will he arrive at his destination? Will those seated get off before he does? Does it matter? Why? Why not?

Where are you headed, traveler?

Entre

When Nurse Light entered the dayroom of the locked ward on Tuesday, Mr. Eberman was masturbating quite openly. Nurse Light walked up to the young vet and remarked, "It must feel good to do that."

"Yes, it surely does," drawled Mr. Eberman with only a short pause in his rhythmical movement.

"Have you had breakfast yet?" wondered the nurse.

"Yes, I have, thank you. Wasn't bad either, for a change." Mr. Eberman looked up for the first time, still grasping but without stroking.

"What did you have this morning?" She sounded interested in this information.

"Sausages and grits. They actually had grits out for us. It's been . . . damn, I don't know how long it's been since we got grits." Both hands were on the arms of the chair pounding lightly to emphasize his point.

"Well, I'm glad to hear it. I like grits too. How do you eat yours?"

Ms. Light was kneeling by the chair now, eyes level with those of Jim Eberman.

"Gravy. Smarley over there puts syrup on his. Ugh!"

"To each his own, I suppose. Mr. Eberman, if you want to continue what you were doing, please do it in the privacy of your room."

"No, I think I'll watch television for a while." Mr. Eberman scooted his chair toward the blaring television set, then he zipped up his pants.

Nurse Light continued making the rounds of her charges.

On Wednesday morning Nurse Tenbraus entered the dayroom to find Mr. Eberman in the midst of flagrant public masturbation. Immediately she told him to stop.

"Why?" he wanted to know without looking up or pausing.

"Because I told you to stop. You know the rules around here. You're no newcomer to this ward. If you don't stop, I'll report you to the doctor."

Mr. Eberman seemed to pick up speed on hearing this threat. He didn't reply.

Nurse Tenbraus raised her voice. Even with the usual high volume of television, everyone in the room could hear her, yet everyone pretended to be in another state.

"If I report you, the doctor will increase your medication. You know that, don't you."

"Huh?"

"You heard me. Stop it, NOW!"

Eberman's body shuddered. He gasped, then he sighed. He smiled and without looking at the nurse, he murmured, "Okay, I'll stop now."

Nurse Tenbraus stomped away unsatisfied. Mr. Eberman began again his long, unsatisfying climb too.

How disappointing for both of them.

References

Fujita, Chihiro. *Morita Therapy*. New York, Tokyo: Igaku-shoin, 1986.

Ishiyama, F. Ishu. "A Case of Severe Test Anxiety Treated in Morita Therapy: Acceptance and Not Fighting It." *Canadian Counsellor* 17 (1983): 172–74.

———. "Current Status of Morita Therapy Research." *International Bulletin of Morita Therapy* 1 (1988): 58–83.

———. "A Japanese Perspective on Client Inaction: Removing Attitudinal Blocks Through Morita Therapy." *Journal of Counseling and Development* 68 (1990): 566–70.

———. "Morita Therapy: Its Basic Features and Cognitive Intervention for Anxiety Treatment." *Psychotherapy* 23 (1986b): 375–81.

———. "Use of Morita Therapy in Shyness Counseling in the West: Promoting Clients' Self-acceptance and Action Taking." *Journal of Counseling and Development* 65 (1987): 547–51.

Kondo, Akihisa. "Morita Therapy: A Japanese Therapy for Neurosis." *American Journal of Psychoanalysis* 13 (1953): 31–37.

Kora, Takehisa; and Ohara, Kenshiro. "Morita Therapy." *Psychology Today* 6, no. 10 (1973): 63–68.

Morita, Masatake. *Seishin Ryoho Kogi.* Tokyo: Hakuyosha, 1983.

Needleman, Jacob. *Lost Christianity.* Garden City, N.Y.: Doubleday, 1980.

Reynolds, David K. *Constructive Living.* Honolulu: University of Hawaii Press, 1984.

―――. *Even in Summer the Ice Doesn't Melt.* New York: William Morrow, 1986.

―――. *Flowing Bridges, Quiet Waters.* Albany: SUNY Press, 1989.

―――. *Morita Psychotherapy.* (English, Japanese, and Spanish editions) Berkeley: University of California Press, 1976a.

―――. "Morita Psychotherapy." In Corsini, R., ed. *Handbook of Innovative Psychotherapies,* pp. 489–501. New York: Wiley, 1981.

―――. "Naikan Psychotherapy." In Corsini, R., ed. *Handbook of Innovative Psychotherapies,* pp. 544–53. New York: Wiley, 1981.

―――. *Naikan Psychotherapy.* Chicago: University of Chicago Press, 1983.

―――. *Playing Ball on Running Water.* New York: William Morrow,1984.

―――. *Pools of Lodging for the Moon.* New York: William Morrow, 1988.

―――. *The Quiet Therapies.* Honolulu: University of Hawaii Press, 1980.

―――. *Thirsty, Swimming in the Lake.* New York: William Morrow, 1991.

―――. *A Thousand Waves.* New York: William Morrow, 1990.

―――. *Water Bears No Scars.* New York: William Morrow, 1987.

Wilhelm, Richard. *Tao Te Ching.* London: Arkana, 1985. (German edition, 1978).

REFERENCES

Information

For information about the nearest Constructive Living instruction and Constructive Living group programs, call:

New York State	(914) 255-3918
New York City	(212) 472-7925
Washington, D.C.	(703) 892-4174
Los Angeles	(213) 389-4088
Chicago	(708) 234-9394
Cleveland	(216) 321-0442
San Francisco	(415) 584-0626

or contact Dr. Reynolds:
Constructive Living
P.O. Box 85
Coos Bay, Oregon 97420
(503) 269-5591

Thirsty, Swimming in the Lake: Essentials of Constructive Living

David K. Reynolds, Ph.D.
The leading authority on Morita therapy shows how to overcome common neuroses such as procrastination, phobias, addictions, and carelessness. Koans, exercises, maxims, case histories, and parables show how life can be lived meaningfully with full attention to doing what needs to be done.
0-688-11032-0

A Thousand Waves: A Sensible Lifestyle for Sensitive People

David K. Reynolds, Ph.D.
"Trying to subdue a wave by striking it only results in a thousand waves" (Morita Masatake). As we try to suppress one feeling, such as shyness or anxiety, we succeed only in generating a thousand others. *A Thousand Waves* is a comprehensive guide to Morita and Naikan, the Japanese ways to more positive living.
0-688-09434-1

Water Bears No Scars

David K. Reynolds, Ph.D.
This is David K. Reynolds's third volume of instruction in the Morita lifeway, the Japanese way to a more constructive, action-based life.
0-688-07448-0

Even in Summer the Ice Doesn't Melt

David K. Reynolds, Ph.D.
Presents the Japanese road to learning to live more constructively and responsibly, written by the leading Western authority on Morita therapy.
0-688-06744-1

Playing Ball on Running Water

David K. Reynolds, Ph.D.
The first popular introduction to a proven Japanese method for helping people reach beyond depression and neurosis to a life of action and accomplishment.
0-688-03913-8

Pools of Lodging for the Moon: Strategies for a Positive Lifestyle

David K. Reynolds, Ph.D.
Through case histories of students, exercises, Zen koans, and instructive fables, Dr. Reynolds shows how to meet the fresh challenges that life brings and how to practice the art of living well from moment to moment.
0-688-11278-1